JAMES ROBISON

WINNING THE REAL WAR

OVERCOMING THE POWER OF DARKNESS

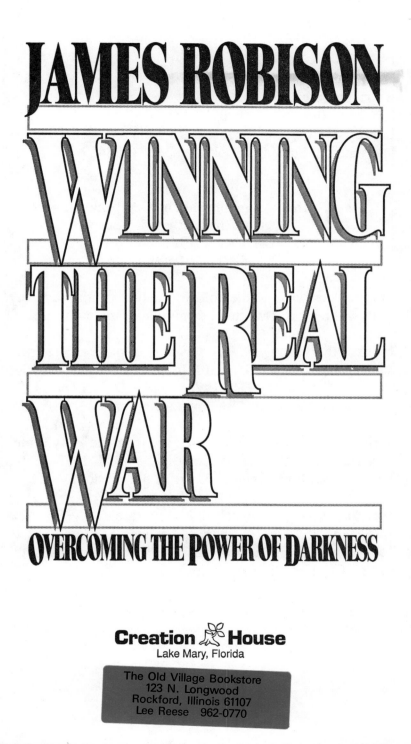

Creation House
Lake Mary, Florida

Creation House
Strang Communications Company
600 Rinehart Road
Lake Mary, FL 32746
(407) 333-0600

*I dedicate this book to my wife, Betty, and my
children, Rhonda, Randy and Robin,
who have learned the reality and necessity
of "winning the real war" by observing
my own spiritual pilgrimage through numerous
defeats and ultimate victory.
I love them with all my heart.*

CONTENTS

5

FOREWORD

WINNING THE REAL WAR ISN'T A book about overcoming an abstract idea of "sin in the world" — sin that is removed from our daily experience. It's about dealing head-on with sin in *us*, the sort of sin that persists and holds us back from fulfilling God's purposes in the world.

Winning the Real War is a book for honest Christians, men and women who take the Bible's demands of holiness seriously. If you read with an open heart, you'll feel challenged to address areas of your life that don't meet God's standards. James Robison takes on our basic temptations: pride, greed, envy, wrath, sloth, lust and gluttony. These "seven deadly sins," as the ancients described them, may have many modern twists that Robison painfully describes. But, writes Robison, their causes and what to do about them are readily available to believers.

I especially like *Winning the Real War* because it's a *real* book. James Robison shares from his experience with remarkable candor. He doesn't preach about your sin so much as he shares about how he has successfully dealt with his own sin. His openness is refreshing in these days of high profile preachers who never quite tell us what's going on in their own lives. You'll know James Robison better after reading this book, and you'll know yourself better too.

Winning the Real War is much more than James Robison's personal experiences. It is biblically grounded teaching that leads the reader along practical steps to the foot of the cross, the true place of forgiveness and victory over all sin.

I guarantee that if you read *Winning the Real War* with an open heart and mind, you won't be the same person. And you'll be better equipped to help others who struggle to live lives pleasing to God.

John Wimber
Yorba Linda, California
February 1991

INTRODUCTION

WHEN IRAQI PRESIDENT SADDAM Hussein invaded Kuwait in August 1990, the stage was set for a major conflict. War became a grim reality as the allied forces, under the leadership of American president George Bush, moved in response to the United Nations resolutions and began the bombardment of Iraq, initiating the liberation

9

of Kuwait.

Long before the first fighter jet took off to release a payload of bombs on its military targets, long before Saddam Hussein moved against the people of Kuwait, the battle had been raging in the heavenlies.

The real war is being waged in the realm of the spirit and in the very heart and soul of every person.

It is this war — both invisible and supernatural — with which we must be primarily concerned. That is the only way we can understand events unfolding in our world and in our lives. This conflict is between the powers of darkness, the kingdom controlled by Satan, and the kingdom of God, controlled by the Lord Jesus and the Holy Spirit.

There are legions of angelic beings, heavenly hosts and demonic spirits which are in continual conflict.

We do have the glorious right and privilege of dispatching angels, defending holy territory, protecting our lives and our families, and assaulting the gates of hell.

We can fight. We must fight. And we can win. We must!

In the midst of this spiritual reality we can actually discern visible characteristics manifested as a result of the invisible activity of satanic powers. Jesus referred to these powers as demons, evil spirits and unclean spirits, and He told us we could cast them out, thereby effectively releasing the power of God's kingdom against Satan.

Surely you have observed certain attitudes and expressions of people manifesting evil-spirit activity. In time such bondage affects even their countenances as well as their actions. You can easily see the spirit of bondage — of anger, of bitterness, of jealousy, of religion and many others — revealed in the faces of people.

You have surely walked into places where you sensed

even atmospherically the presence of evil. Sadly, you can feel this same presence in many religious settings. Various denominations have controlling spirits. Some seem to have the spirit of slumber or complacency, others the spirit of death and still others of hype and excess.

Upon entering a home, you may sense either abiding peace or an underlying tension. You can visit various cities and states, as well as regions and nations, and discern the prevailing spirits. In Mexico, for example, you will likely sense a heavy spirit of oppression and depression. Visiting Canada, you will immediately discern the spirit of tradition which has bound many people and kept them from the freedom they could experience in Christ. In our own United States the spirits of rebellion, self-centeredness, materialism and indulgence are easily detected.

It is my prayer that through the reading of this book you will be made keenly aware of the reality of the invisible kingdom and the war continually raging in this invisible realm. We are in a battle for which most people have never shown up; some do not even know there is a war.

As believers we have been called to be good soldiers of the Lord Jesus Christ, to "fight the good fight of faith" and to be "more than conquerors" in this life.[1]

Recent events related to the war in the Persian Gulf illustrate in the physical realm what believers and the church of Jesus Christ must now experience in the spiritual realm.

The victorious allied forces moved in true unity in spite of differences. They were diverse but they became one and thus became a powerful force against evil enemy activity.

The church must become one in purpose and in Christ, moving in true spiritual unity, in order to win against the forces of Satan.

11

The allied forces used an all-out air assault to pave the way to victory. So must the church pray in the power of the Holy Spirit and storm the heavenlies in intercession. Pray in a spiritual air assault.

Then the armored assault followed with tanks and artillery. So must the Christian put on the whole armor of God and move against Satan. The air and artillery assault was followed by the infantry in hand-to-hand combat which was minimal, as were the casualties. After praying and putting on the armor, the true believers must confront Satan without fear. The church storms the gates of hell and sets captives free just as the allied forces liberated Kuwait.

One of the greatest truths concerning the kingdom is the promise that we can be overcomers and set others free. This is the gospel of the kingdom. We are called not only to overcome the temptations of this world, but the powers of darkness which control so much of this world's activity and far too much of our own lives. Remember Christ desires to establish His kingdom, His rule in the lives of individual believers. He rules in our lives regardless of who controls the lives of others in this world.

For years I did not understand the reality of the real war and did not know the necessity of fighting and winning in spiritual warfare. As a result of often walking in spiritual darkness, I lost Christian victory and nearly lost my ministry, my health and my very life.

What I share in this book is the result of diligent pursuit of scriptural truth and my own personal experience of defeat and ultimate victory over the forces of darkness.

James Robison
February 1991

ONE

THE REALITY OF THE SPIRIT WORLD

THE CRUSADE MEETING HAD BEEN exhausting, and I was eager to get back to my hotel room. I never imagined what God had in store for me that night.

I had often read Paul's injunction in Philippians 4:8 to think on things that are "honorable...right...pure... lovely...of good repute," but those kinds of thoughts were being crowded out. The devil's thoughts lodged in my mind, filling me with bitterness and hostility. I was judgmental and critical and constantly tried to shape people into the image of my desires, rather than allow them to become the people God planned for them to be. I struggled against lust, outbursts of anger and an uncontrollable appetite. But the harder I fought, the tighter the bonds squeezed me. I longed to be free, yet knew I was not. Even worse, I lived the life of a hypocrite.

I called my close friend and associate Dudley Hall at 1:00 A.M. the next morning. "Dudley, can a person be free? Do you know anyone who is really free?"

Not long afterward Dudley put me in contact with Milton Green. Milton was no well-known evangelist. He was a carpet cleaner who loved Jesus and knew his authority in Christ. Desperate, I invited Milton to fly with me to an upcoming crusade. On the trip down he shared from the Word with undeniable power and authority. That night after the meeting I invited him back to my hotel room to share further. We talked a while, then Milton looked over at me.

"I've been listening to you and praying for you six years," he said. "I feel so sorry for you. I believe you're the most demon-assaulted person I've ever seen. You're so tormented I don't know how you've kept your sanity."

He was right. I was tormented in my mind and miserable. Even though I had a very large ministry, I knew I was living in personal defeat and bondage. Thank God, I was willing to admit it and cry out for help.

Milton asked if he could pray for me. I said yes, and he laid his hands on my shoulders and confessed who we as believers are in Christ. He acknowledged the defeat in my life, and I agreed with him in that prayer. Walking around the room, he then began to rebuke the evil spirits that were attacking me: spirits of criticism, anger, compulsion and lust. His voice boomed with authority and, as he boldly commanded the spirits to leave, they left.

I didn't understand it — didn't even know it had happened until forty-eight hours later when I awakened with Scripture verses flowing from my lips and from a clear mind.

When this humble carpet cleaner battled the forces of darkness, using his authority in Christ, the chains that bound me fell away. By my own efforts I had been unable to live in victory; through spiritual authority I was set free. I was truly delivered from recurring defeat and bondage.

Is There Really a War Going on?

"Spiritual warfare? What's that?"

Many Christians respond with shock and confusion whenever this very real subject is brought up. Others are misinformed and therefore easily deceived. Still others regard it as so much nonsense. But the Bible leaves no room for debate: Spiritual warfare is real — and the battle is raging.

At the end of his letter to the Christians at Ephesus, the apostle Paul says this:

> Finally, be strong in the Lord, and in the strength of His might. Put on the full armor of God, that you may be able to stand firm against the schemes of the devil. For our struggle is not against flesh and blood, but against the rulers, against the powers, against the world forces of this darkness,

against the spiritual forces of wickedness in the heavenly places (Eph. 6:10-12).

An invisible spiritual world exists, and it affects us and everything around us. In an eternal sense, this unseen realm is the stage on which the real drama of our lives is carried out. It is where our conflicts originate — conflicts that spill over into the visible, physical, temporal world.

Focus on Jesus

Before we go further in our discussion of spiritual warfare, let me emphasize the importance of keeping our focus on Jesus Christ, not Satan. I will be sharing many biblical principles, but these truths alone will not lead you to victory. They are tools to move us toward godliness. But the clearest demonstration of godliness was found in the life of Jesus Christ. You will find victory in spiritual warfare only when you set your mind and emotions on the sufficiency of Christ's sacrifice for your sins. Allowing the power of Jesus to change your thoughts, habits and character is the key to overcoming the evil one.

Paul reminds us in Colossians, "For in Him all the fulness of Deity dwells in bodily form, and in Him you have been made complete, and He is the head over all rule and authority" (Col. 2:9-10).

The writer of Hebrews echoes this thought:

> God, after He spoke long ago to the fathers in the prophets in many portions and in many ways, in these last days has spoken to us in His Son, whom He appointed heir of all things, through whom

also He made the world. And He is the radiance of His glory and the exact representation of His nature (Heb. 1:1-3).

It all boils down to a relationship with Jesus. Only He can teach you, through the Holy Spirit, how to apply truth to particular situations. He'll give you truths that will equip you to defeat the enemy.

Satan was defeated at the cross. When you die to self and are raised to newness of life in Jesus, you can have the mind, the grace, the power and the authority of Christ. Thus you are empowered to walk over all the enemy. This is what Paul was talking about when he wrote:

> For we do not preach ourselves but Christ Jesus as Lord....But we have this treasure in earthen vessels, that the surpassing greatness of the power may be of God and not from ourselves....Therefore we do not lose heart....For momentary, light affliction is producing for us an eternal weight of glory far beyond all comparison, while we look not at the things which are seen, but at the things which are not seen; for the things which are seen are temporal, but the things which are not seen are eternal (2 Cor. 4:5,7,16-18).

Paul knew that the unseen spiritual world was the ultimate reality and that the presence of Christ in his life gave him final victory. That's why he could say the things he suffered were a "momentary, light affliction."

Paul had learned the most important fact of all: Jesus is Lord! The victory is already won! Now, keeping that in mind, let's go on. What is spiritual warfare, and how does it affect us?

How the Battle Affects Our Lives

Every area of your life involves spiritual warfare — your personal relationships, your relationship with Christ, your career, your worship and service in the church, even your attitudes about yourself. You and I are under attack.

My ministry frequently utilizes electronic devices to aid communication, such as radio, television and cassette tapes. When I'm broadcasting from a television station in the Dallas/Ft. Worth metroplex, the broadcast signal shares the airwaves with more than forty other TV signals as well as dozens of radio stations.

I've never understood how an invisible, inaudible television signal can be sent hundreds of miles through the air, and then someone sitting in their living room can turn a dial or push a button and get a clear picture. I understand only one thing about the process: If you want to receive the signal, you have to tune it in.

The spiritual world is similar. It sends out invisible signals that can reach into our lives. The quality of our lives depends on which of these spiritual signals we receive, or "tune in," or learn to "tune out."

The great tragedy of the human condition is that we are born with a damaged spiritual "receiver." Apart from Jesus Christ we are "by nature children of wrath" (Eph. 2:3). We remain such until we're born of the Spirit through an encounter with Jesus. As "children of wrath" we're naturally in communication with the forces of spiritual darkness. Consequently we never had to be taught to do wrong.

Our beautiful little granddaughter always looks so angelic when she is sleeping. But when she's awake and acting out of control, ignoring all her parents' instructions, it's evident that she is tuning into the wrong signal — signals from her sin nature, even signals from spiritual forces of darkness.

I have a vivid memory of one time when her dad was trying to get her to apologize for something. She didn't want to say "I'm sorry." Instead, she said, "Daddy, it's tough." He was asking her to make a morally correct decision, and her response was, "It's tough."

What is this conflict that affects even a child? I'm convinced it's spiritual warfare. All the terrible things in our visible world have an invisible component. Spiritual forces behind the scenes create discord and violence and encourage self-serving corruption. As Paul said in Ephesians 6:12, "our struggle is not against flesh and blood, but against...the world forces of this darkness." We're in the midst of a very real battle.

Satan attacks the church, and we write it off as normal disagreement. He attacks our families, and we label it unavoidable conflict. He attacks us directly, and we assume it's personal weakness.

Spiritual forces are attracting considerable attention in the secular media. Satanism, occult rituals, witchcraft and satanic sacrifice are front-page news. If the secular press recognizes the reality of the devil's influence, surely it is time Christians take it more seriously.

Satan Attacks the Church

We've all watched as major ministries have been torn apart by scandals involving money, sex and power. Leading pastors are dragged into sin and corruption. Sad to say, the enemy has a death-grip on the life of much of the church.

In the second and third chapters of Revelation, we see Jesus evaluating seven of the earliest churches in Asia Minor (modern Turkey). Five of the seven were told to clean up their acts. Not only did they need to repent, but they needed to overcome. Some had sound doctrine, some stood against the world, but they all had left their first love. They no longer possessed a pure devotion to Jesus. They were losing the battle of the mind and living in defeat. To all of them Jesus was saying what He said to the church in Laodicea: "He who overcomes, I will grant to him to sit down with Me on My throne, as I also overcame and sat down with My Father on His throne" (Rev. 3:21). He wanted His people to be overcomers. He wants us in the church today to be overcomers too.

Satan Attacks the Family

Satan doesn't limit his influence to the church. Our families are also under attack. The things that damage your family relationships are not just unfortunate coincidences. Evil spirits are working to divide you from those you love. The Bible teaches that Satan is the accuser of the brethren; he wants your family life disrupted through mutual accusation.

Satan is also a murderer. He works to kill you and those you love through slander, malice and dissension. He does it through abuse, neglect and self-centeredness, or drugs and alcohol. His goal is to take away the life and vitality of the family. One of his most effective ploys is to attack each member of the family on an individual basis.

Satan Attacks Individual Believers

If you are skeptical about Satan's ability to attack individual believers, consider the following passages from the New Testament.

Early in Jesus' ministry, when the disciples asked Him to teach them how to pray, He included this petition in His model prayer: "...and do not lead us into temptation, but deliver us from evil [or the evil one]" (Matt. 6:13). Why would He tell His disciples to pray this way if the evil one couldn't bother believers?

In Luke 22:31-32 Jesus warns Peter: "Simon, Simon, behold, Satan has demanded permission to sift you like wheat; but I have prayed for you, that your faith may not fail; and you, when once you have turned again, strengthen your brothers." Why did Jesus say this to Peter if the devil couldn't affect him?

Just before the crucifixion Peter denied Jesus three times. Do you think that was the Holy Ghost influencing him? No, it was a most unholy ghost. It was an evil spirit.

In John 17 we find Jesus' longest recorded prayer, which follows the Last Supper. In it He prays first for Himself, then for the disciples who were there at the table with Him. Finally He prays for all the people who will come to believe in Him throughout human history.

In verse 15 Jesus makes this statement about the disciples: "I do not ask Thee to take them out of the world, but to keep them from the evil one." Jesus knew His disciples would be exposed to Satan's influence as long as they were living in the world.

Later, in the book of First Peter, we find these words written by an older and much wiser Simon Peter: "Be of sober spirit, be on the alert. Your adversary, the devil, prowls about like a roaring lion, seeking someone to devour" (1 Pet. 5:8).

The Bible talks about Satan as an adversary and warns that he disguises himself as an angel of light (2 Cor. 11:14). The Bible also mentions evil spirit beings who seek to impress their personalities and priorities on human beings. They are the tools Satan uses to thwart Christians.

I am not saying Christians can be demon-possessed. Demonic spirits cannot totally control Christians, because we have been internally changed by the Holy Spirit. We can resist; we can overcome; we can go for help. But please understand: Christians can be demon-assaulted — oppressed and defeated by demonic attacks.

Evil spirit forces will try to influence you through a spirit of fear, rebellion or intimidation. You may be troubled by spirits of inferiority, rejection or deception. You may find your attempts to serve Christ blocked by spirits of tradition or pride. A spirit of hate, hostility, dissension or discord may interfere with your relationships.

Satanic influence, expressed through demonic oppression, can establish strongholds in our lives, partially controlling us and distorting the shape of our character. Some spiritual forces can literally overwhelm us. We have all seen this happen. Christians do things totally out of character, becoming angry, corrupt, malicious or deeply depressed. We wonder what is going on. It's the reality of spiritual warfare.

Summary

All born-again believers are involved in a spiritual warfare whether they know it or not. This battle rages in the invisible realm, which is in fact the "real" world. The enemy, Satan, attacks the church, the family and the individual believer. He uses hordes of evil spirits — demons — to carry out his assault. In this book you will find many biblical directives for standing against the enemy and living victoriously. Your primary strategy, however, is to keep your focus on Jesus. Only through an intimate, personal relationship with Him will you be able to overcome all the schemes of Satan.

T W O

KNOW THE ENEMY

ONE OF THE HARDEST ANIMALS TO hunt is the trophy white-tail deer. One misty day I had been sitting motionless for hours in the woods, hidden, watching a herd of these deer. A doe appeared. She couldn't have known I was there. Everything was still, and I was not upwind from her. Suddenly she stiffened. Her white tail drew up tight against her buttocks. She sensed danger.

The doe looked around. Her eyes froze. Her tail shot straight back. She knew an enemy was nearby. As I studied this beautiful creature, I asked God, "How does she know? Why is she so smart?"

"She's not smart. She's alert," God replied. "That's what makes these deer so hard to hunt. From the day they are born almost everything around them — coyotes, bobcats and lions — tries to kill them, and they know it. They stay alert to stay alive."

In a sense, you and I are a lot like those deer. From the day we are born Satan schemes to claim our souls. From the time we are born again he works to destroy our testimonies and our lives. The tragic part is, unlike the white-tail deer, we too often don't know it. We are not alert.

Satan is very crafty. To overcome him we must learn to be spiritually alert. This doesn't mean harboring an undue awareness of the enemy. Rather spiritual alertness grows out of a total consciousness of Christ — loving God with all our heart.

Nonetheless, winning any victory requires knowledge of how the enemy works. What is our enemy like? What is Satan doing?

The Nature of Satan

Some argue that we shouldn't try to discuss Satan in great detail because the Bible's information about him is too sketchy to construct an accurate picture. I don't agree. We have enough information to know our enemy well, if we apply ourselves to that task.

Revelation 12 is often interpreted as an historical description of activity both in the spiritual world and the visible world. It begins with the birth of Jesus and includes His resurrection and return to a position of honor and authority in heaven. The chapter even includes some comments about the nature and activity of Satan. Consider verses 7-9:

> And there was war in heaven, Michael and his angels waging war with the dragon. And the dragon and his angels waged war, and they were not strong enough, and there was no longer a place found for them in heaven. And the great dragon was thrown down, the serpent of old who is called the devil and Satan, who deceives the whole world; he was thrown down to the earth, and his angels were thrown down with him.

Though the description is complex, the basic message is straightforward: Satan is a strong and dangerous enemy; he is stronger than we are by ourselves — but not stronger than we are in combination with Christ.

Luke 10 has more to tell us about this. Jesus had sent a large group of His disciples out to proclaim the kingdom of God:

> And the seventy returned with joy, saying, "Lord, even the demons are subject to us in Your name." And He said to them, "I was watching Satan fall from heaven like lightning. Behold, I have given you authority to tread upon serpents and scorpions, and over all the power of the enemy, and nothing shall injure you. Nevertheless do not rejoice in this, that the spirits are subject to you,

but rejoice that your names are recorded in heaven" (Luke 10:17-20).

Satan and his demons are actually subject to us as we follow Jesus! We have been given authority "over all the power of the enemy." We may be assaulted, but we need not be overcome. We have authority to wage spiritual warfare in the name of Jesus.

Unwittingly, some Christians talk about Satan as if he were as powerful as God. He isn't. Satan is a created being with limited power. For example, he can be in only one place at a time. To extend his influence, he must find others to act as his agents.

In the Gospel of Matthew Jesus identifies some of these allies when He calls Satan the ruler of demons (Matt. 12:22-28). The account given in Revelation portrays Satan leading his allies in warfare. There are many combatants in this cosmic struggle. God's angels are actively involved in warfare, as are "the dragon and his angels" (Rev. 12:7), or Satan and his demons.

The Character of Satan

Satan's primary characteristic is self-centeredness. His basic motivation is always to exalt himself, to gain mastery, to rule in the place of God. This self-centered nature is clearly revealed in Isaiah 14:12-14:

> "How you have fallen from heaven, O star of the morning, son of the dawn! You have been cut down to the earth, you who have weakened the nations! But you said in your heart, 'I will ascend

to heaven; I will raise my throne above the stars
of God, and I will sit on the mount of assembly
in the recesses of the north. I will ascend above
the heights of the clouds; I will make myself like
the Most High.' "

In His description of Satan, Jesus reveals that this self-
centered fallen angel will stop at nothing to attain his evil
objectives.

First, Jesus tells us Satan is a liar and the father of all
lies (John 8:42-47). He is the motivating force behind all
deception and deceiving spirits. When we slander others
and treat them maliciously, we are playing the devil's game.

Second, Satan is a thief. He takes away the spirit of love
and gives a spirit of criticism. In John 10 Jesus depicts
Himself as the good Shepherd who gives up His life for the
sheep (v. 11). Satan is portrayed as the robber who tries to
steal and molest the sheep (John 10:1-18). He robs us of
joy, peace and love. He steals our loyalty to God through
secularism or religious idolatry.

Third, Jesus says Satan is a murderer (John 8:44). He
assassinates people's character through false accusations or
suggestions.

Fourth, the Bible identifies Satan as the accuser of the
brethren (Rev. 12:10). He wants you to accuse people —
anyone will do. He will deceive you, making you puff up
with spiritual pride in the midst of your accusation. You
may even grow comfortable with accusing. Soon slander
will be a normal part of your life, and you will justify it
with all sorts of corrupt theological tricks.

Above all else, Satan is a deceiver. In 2 Corinthians 11
Paul has some important things to say about how Satan

29

presents his lies to us:

> But I am afraid, lest as the serpent deceived Eve
> by his craftiness, your minds should be led astray
> from the simplicity and purity of devotion to
> Christ. For if one comes and preaches another
> Jesus whom we have not preached, or you receive
> a different spirit which you have not received, or
> a different gospel which you have not ac-
> cepted....[Know that] such men are false apos-
> tles, deceitful workers, disguising themselves as
> apostles of Christ....Even Satan disguises himself
> as an angel of light. Therefore it is not surprising
> if his servants also disguise themselves as servants
> of righteousness (vv. 3-4, 13-15).

Satan seeks to lead us away from "purity of devotion to
Christ" (v. 3). He tries to lure us into following someone
who "preaches another Jesus" (v. 4), such as a compas-
sionless, legalistic Jesus. It is a lie. Always remember, Satan
is a master of disguise.

In Revelation 2 Jesus, speaking through the apostle John,
gives an example of a deceitful worker who is leading
Christians away from Himself:

> "But I have this against you, that you tolerate the
> woman Jezebel, who calls herself a prophetess,
> and she teaches and leads My bond-servants
> astray, so that they commit acts of immorality and
> eat things sacrificed to idols....But I say to
> you...who do not hold this teaching, who have not
> known the deep things of Satan...I place no other

burden on you" (vv. 20,24).

Jezebel called herself a "prophetess" (v. 20). She wanted to be recognized as an authority figure, so she bestowed a powerful title on herself. False teachers always want to make a name for themselves; they want to wield authority without exercising discipline or sharing in suffering.

Jezebel's teaching involved self-indulgence. She apparently encouraged the sexually immoral "worship" activities common in certain pagan temples at that time.

Finally, she encouraged Christians to seek esoteric, "hidden" truth, truth that only a select few may attain. Many mysterious religious cults threatened the early church's stability with promises of supernatural experiences, unlimited power or special revelations. Jezebel even openly referred to the origins of these "deep things of Satan" (v. 24).

The apostle John also had much to say about those who are influenced by Satan's lies:

> Children, it is the last hour; and just as you heard that antichrist is coming, even now many antichrists have arisen....They went out from us, but they were not really of us; for if they had been of us, they would have remained with us....Who is the liar but the one who denies that Jesus is the Christ? This is the antichrist, the one who denies the Father and the Son (1 John 2:18-19,22).

Satan works through the deceptions of the antichrists, those who masquerade as servants of Jesus when they actually are trying to push Him aside. They become leaders in religious communities and organizations, yet they deny what the Bible teaches about Jesus as both true man and true God. They inspire disagreement, dissension and division. Their teachings and actions result in damaged and disillusioned people. Such people are often controlled or influenced by demonic forces. They use the same words Jesus would use, but they distort the meaning of those words.

The Strategy of Satan

Satan's character gives us a clue to his strategies for distracting us from Jesus. He is a created being; he cannot create anything new. So to carry out his plan of spiritual subversion he must use what God has created.

The devil is a master counterfeiter, and he loves to tamper with the gospel, for example. Paul addressed that problem in his letter to the Galatians. The Christians there had been exposed to the teaching of people called Judaizers. These were Jewish Christians who taught that after you accepted Jesus as Savior, you had to conform your life-style to the standards of the Law of Moses. That sounded good to the people because it fit in with cultural expectations and emphasized self-discipline. Thus the Judaizers created a new gospel by adding to the original teaching of Jesus. Satan didn't create the gospel, but he could mix in additions from the Jewish law.

To be successful at controlling what God has created, Satan must hide his purposes as much as possible. This was his strategy with Eve. Regarding the tree of the knowledge of good and evil, he said to her, "You surely shall not die! For God knows that in the day you eat from it your eyes will be opened, and you will be like God, knowing good and evil" (Gen. 3:4b,5).

Satan acted as if he wanted to help Eve become like God. His real purpose was to separate Eve from God by leading her into a kind of idolatry: the worship of the knowledge of good and evil. Anytime we worship something in place of God, we damage our relationship with Him and cut ourselves off from the source of our life. That suits Satan just fine, because that's when he can influence us.

Satan used idolatry to influence God's people in both the Old and the New Testament. Consider these verses that describe the relationship between God and His people:

> "They made Him jealous with strange gods; with abominations they provoked Him to anger. They sacrificed to demons who were not God, to gods whom they have not known, new gods who came lately, whom your fathers did not dread. You neglected the Rock who begot you, and forgot the God who gave you birth" (Deut. 32:16-18).

In this passage Moses, the great lawgiver of the Old Testament, is speaking to the assembled people of Israel shortly before his death. The people of God are about to enter the promised land, and Moses is warning them that they will abandon God. They would soon fall into Satan's trap, become idol worshippers and even make sacrifices to demons.

God uses Israel and the Old Testament to teach us spiritual lessons and truths. Paul said in 1 Corinthians 10:6, "These things happened as examples for us." Israel's struggles can teach us how to win spiritual battles.

Paul refers to Israel's experiences and then gives a warning to Christians:

> Therefore let him who thinks he stands take heed lest he fall. No temptation has overtaken you but such as is common to man; and God is faithful, who will not allow you to be tempted beyond what you are able, but with the temptation will provide the way of escape also, that you may be able to endure it. Therefore, my beloved, flee from idolatry....I do not want you to become sharers in demons. You cannot drink the cup of the Lord and the cup of demons; you cannot partake of the table of the Lord and the table of demons (1 Cor. 10:12-14,20-21).

When you sacrifice to something, you are worshipping it. In so doing you become sharers with demons rather than sharers in the fullness of blessing and truth of the Spirit. You may not make burnt offerings, but you do make sacrifices. You put your time, money and energy into your idols. When you do this, you are working with demons and supporting their cause.

Satan's final strategy is found in another part of Revelation 12:

> And I heard a loud voice in heaven, saying, "Now the salvation, and the power, and the kingdom of our God and the authority of His Christ have come, for the accuser of our brethren has been thrown down....And they overcame him because of the blood of the Lamb and because of the word

of their testimony, and they did not love their life even to death....Rejoice, O heavens and you who dwell in them. Woe to the earth and the sea, because the devil has come down to you, having great wrath, knowing that he has only a short time (vv. 10-12).

Satan was accusing the people of God before Christ appeared on the earth. Jesus brought the salvation, power and authority of God's kingdom into the world, but Satan continues his practice of accusation. In fact, he does it with even greater wrath and urgency because he has seen the dawn of his final defeat in the establishment of the kingdom of God through the church.

Historically, Christians identify three basic enemies of the kingdom of God: the world, the flesh and the devil. The world is the fallen world system with its ways of thinking, feeling and acting that threaten to rob the beauty of Jesus from our lives. The flesh is a term for the parts of our character that do not yet look like Jesus. It pressures us from the inside and can corrupt our behavior. We believe in the world and the flesh; we can identify and understand these "enemies."

Belief in the devil is a different matter. In the last two hundred years our increasing dependence on rationalism and materialism has blinded us to invisible spiritual realities. Rationalism tells us to trust what we can observe and analyze. Materialism tells us to draw our data from the visible world. Neither leaves room for the devil. Many have forgotten about the devil, but he has not forgotten about us.

The Bible warns that spiritual conflict is caused by more than just the world and the flesh. There is another influence, another player on the stage of human history. There is more going on in our lives, our world and our churches than can be explained by what we can observe and analyze. The battle is raging all around us in the unseen spiritual realm — and our real enemy is Satan and his demons.

Summary

In any war, knowing the enemy's true identity and having the ability to recognize him and his activities are essential to victory. Our war in the spiritual realm is no exception. The Bible clearly identifies our enemy as Satan. It describes his nature, his character and his strategy. By becoming aware of these facts about the enemy, we can prepare ourselves and be alert for his attempts to defeat us.

THREE

SATAN ATTACKS
THE CHURCH

The church today is falling
prey to the same deception that trapped Eve. We define
ourselves by our theology, ethics and institutions. We rely
on rules, regulations and regimentation. We have a form of
godliness, but we're dying inside because we won't let
God's Spirit work within us to build the body of Christ.

37

Division in the Church

Paul knew the church in Corinth was in trouble. He noted two critical signs of this in his letter: conflict and pride (1 Cor. 1:10-13). Some of the believers at Corinth claimed to follow Paul, others were loyal to Apollos, some preferred Peter — and some even boasted that they alone followed Jesus. In allowing these divisions to develop, the people had lost touch with the real Jesus.

I remember one time when I met with the pastor of a church to prepare for a revival. He launched into a tirade against a fellow preacher in the town. As he talked on and on about what a fraud and hypocrite this brother in Christ was, my heart sank. When I left his office, I was sick in my soul. The Jesus that man had shown me was not the Jesus I wanted people to receive.

Satan and his allies are behind the bitter divisions that afflict the church today. They foster the beliefs that we have a Baptist Jesus, a Methodist Jesus, a Pentecostal Jesus and a charismatic Jesus. Yet Paul said anyone who preaches any other Jesus than the real Jesus is accursed (Gal. 1:6-9).

Within most churches real openness and warmth are rare, and contact between churches is often nonexistent. The family of God is fractured and fragmented, divided and divisive. This is not what Jesus had in mind when He said, "By this all men will know that you are My disciples, if you have love for one another" (John 13:35).

My heart breaks because Christians have so little true love for one another. What love there is often is misdirected, causing people to become more devoted to their denomination, ministry, reputation or image than to God.

Worshipping Churches Rather Than Christ

The people of God in the Old Testament had been deceived. They had come to believe that the temple building and the sacrificial system associated with it gave them guaranteed access to God. As long as they protected the structure and its ceremonies, God would have to protect them.

Christians today often make the same mistake about their church buildings, programs and denominations. They assume that as long as the machinery of ministry is intact, then spiritual life must be flowing out of it. God says such ideas are "deceptive words" (Jer. 7:4,8).

When the focus of our worship drifts away from God, we have fallen into idolatry. The prophet Jeremiah spent his entire adult life speaking out against the idolatry of God's people. We can learn something about our folly and danger by examining his words:

> Thus says the Lord of hosts, the God of Israel, "Amend your ways and your deeds, and I will let you dwell in this place. Do not trust in deceptive words, saying, 'This is the temple of the Lord'....Behold, you are trusting in deceptive words to no avail. Will you steal, murder, and commit adultery, and swear falsely, and offer sacrifices to Baal, and walk after other gods that you have not known, then come and stand before Me in this house, which is called by My name, and say, 'We are delivered!'...? Has this house, which is called by My name, become a den of robbers in your sight?" (Jer. 7:3-4, 8-11a).

The Israelites were making sacrifices to many different gods to ensure their safety and prosperity. They pursued idolatry to gain some control over their lives. When we focus our attention on things other than Jesus — even religious things — it's usually for similar reasons. And the results are the same. Then, as now, the house of God will be full of thieves, robbers, self-seekers and merchandisers of religion.

This is what God had to say about their situation:

> "But go now to My place which was in Shiloh, where I made My name dwell at the first, and see what I did to it because of the wickedness of My people Israel. And now, because you have done all these things," declares the Lord, "and I spoke to you...but you did not hear, and I called you but you did not answer, therefore, I will do to the house which is called by My name, in which you trust, and to the place which I gave you and your fathers, as I did to Shiloh. And I will cast you out of My sight, as I have cast out all your brothers, all the offspring of Ephraim" (Jer. 7:12-15).

God made an example out of Shiloh. That was the place where He was first worshipped after Israel entered the promised land, the place where His glory was shown to the people. But they responded to His love with treachery and ignored His instructions about living and worship. What angered Him most, though, were the "high places" where they worshipped other gods; their greatest treachery involved corrupt religious institutions.

Never forget that some demons are religious spirits. Satan

quoted Scripture in tempting Jesus, and his demons are adept at using the Bible and religious issues to create turmoil and division in the body of Christ. Many of us have provoked God by exalting our denominations and religious institutions. We have fallen victim to religious spirits. We have become captives to Christian idolatry — we desperately need to be set free.

Demonic religious spirits work to keep Christians bound. They strive to prevent us from fulfilling the Great Commission by closing our ears to God. Instead, we hear only the words of our favorite pastor, evangelist, teacher or denominational leader.

Pastor Francis Frangipane has accurately stated, "A religious spirit while honoring God's works in the past will resist His works in the present."[1]

Nothing would thrill me more than to see the church united in love and living in the strength and victory God meant for it. In many Christian circles, however, the idea of Christian unity is met with closed ears and hearts of stone. Some who were closest to me in the past respond with a blank stare or a condescending smile when I talk about deliverance from religious idolatry and demonic influence in the church. Many are bitterly defensive and openly hostile to these ideas.

If you embrace the unity of the body of Christ, you can expect the same reactions. You may get a stony silence. If you press your point, you will probably encounter defensiveness. Don't worry about what the religious crowd says. Don't commit religious idolatry by seeking the approval of people more than the approval of God. Don't worry even if you are put out of some church. You can't be forced out of the true church! Paul warned the Corinthians that their idolatry was destroying them. They were becoming spiritually linked to demons and bringing God's judgment on themselves (1 Cor. 10:14-22; 11:27-32). If you get kicked out of that kind of environment, you should thank God!

One of the leading pastors in a Pentecostal denomination and his son, who also was a pastor, attended one of our Bible conferences a few years ago. One night the glory of God settled on twelve thousand people. There were women lifting their hands to the Lord and dancing before Him. People were speaking with other tongues. These two men should have been perfectly comfortable in that environment. They weren't. They saw the makeup and jewelry many of the women wore and were offended. The younger preacher turned to his father and said, "Dad, what do you think?" The older man replied, "Son, I think we're in trouble." He saw the glory of God touching people, but he couldn't accept it as real because the women wore jewelry and makeup. His theology would not allow him to receive what God was doing.

We let religious institutions and traditions cause us to lose sight of what God is doing through the whole body of Christ. We must learn to respect each other and listen to one another — even those who differ from our little group. We need each other.

Surviving the assault of our adversary, who is prowling like a lion, requires concentration on the whole Word of God. We can't just focus on the parts that are theologically attractive to us. If we do, Satan will keep us divided.

When we let other Christians help us read the Bible honestly, with a heart of compassion and a will to obey, it will expand our limited theology and overcome our dead traditions. It will also drive out the enemy.

The Bible can be our best defense against religious idolatry — but only if we study it together and learn from each other rather than use it as a textbook for theological warfare. Look at Paul's advice about this to Timothy:

> Remind them of these things, and solemnly charge them in the presence of God not to wrangle about words, which is useless, and leads to the ruin of the hearers. Be diligent to present yourself approved to God as a workman who does not need to be ashamed, handling accurately the word of truth. But avoid worldly and empty chatter, for it will lead to further ungodliness, and their talk will spread like gangrene....Now flee from youthful lusts, and pursue righteousness, faith, love and peace....But refuse foolish and ignorant speculations, knowing that they produce quarrels. And the Lord's bond-servant must not be quarrelsome, but be kind to all, able to teach, patient when wronged, with gentleness correcting those who are in opposition, if perhaps...they may come to their senses and escape from the snare of the devil (2 Tim. 2:14-17a, 22-26).

Vicious theological disputes destroy "the hearers" (v. 14). All who take part in such conflicts lose. Theological orthodoxy will not protect us from satanic influence if we use it as a weapon for personal conquest. When we handle the Scriptures properly, we are drawing the life of God from them. That life will change us into the image of Christ. If we have stopped looking like Jesus, it's likely the life of God is no longer flowing from the Scriptures into our lives.

If our theological positions make us mean and intolerant, they are nothing but "foolish and ignorant speculations" (v. 23). If our study of the Bible does not produce the fruit of the Spirit (Gal. 5:22-26), then we are destroying the truth rather than establishing it.

Do not underestimate Satan's ability to hold a religious institution captive through the theological pride of its members. We have far too many churches that are fortresses from which pastor/generals conduct campaigns against other parts of the Christian community. This is not of God. It's true that, as defenders of the truth, part of our job is to rebuke, reprove and correct. But we must do it with gentleness and long-suffering in the hope that people will "come to their senses and escape...the devil" (v. 26). Theological pride will only bring us, and others, to destruction through accusation, jealousy and ambition.

Accusing Other Christians

Jesus prayed that the church would be one as He and the Father are one (John 17:11; compare with vv. 6-12). Satan's strategy is to destroy the unity of the body of Christ by stirring us to accuse other believers. This is one of the most insidious results of theological pride.

We all know the church is not yet perfect because Christians are not perfect people. We are forgiven; we have opportunities to grow; but we do not always look like Jesus.

When a problem surfaces, Satan and his minions jump to exploit it. They hold it up gleefully for everyone to see, analyzing it and whispering about exactly how bad it is. They accuse everyone in sight of being responsible for it, leaving people with no hope for a solution.

Jesus takes a very different approach. He sees the problem, then He joins us in our suffering and intercedes for us with the Father. He sends the Holy Spirit, who is called the Comforter, to support us and help us solve the problem. Jesus died and rose again to make us overcomers; He replaces Satan's accusations with redemption.

When we see a problem in the church, we must choose which of these examples we want to follow. We can follow Satan by accusing our fellow believers, or we can follow Jesus and discover the redemptive purposes of God.

One manifestation of my bondage to darkness was the accusatory anger I spewed onto my brothers and sisters in Christ. I often felt the power of the Holy Spirit when I preached. On other occasions a great hostility would wash over me. Satan would lie to me, saying, "God wants you to tell them off." He tricked me into thinking it was the righteous thing to do, but such "righteous indignation" is not from God — because human anger cannot create the righteousness God desires (James 1:20).

During one angry outburst before a group of seminary professors I made some broad accusations. I condemned them as liberal theologians and accused them of diluting and distorting the Word of God.

After my deliverance God showed me I was wrong to attack them as a body. I wept for the hurt I had caused. At the earliest opportunity I went back before that group and asked for their forgiveness. I was right to stand against liberal trends that cause doubt and unbelief in the Scriptures, but I was wrong to lash out in anger, painting many with a broad brush of criticism.

Jealousy and Selfish Ambition

> Who among you is wise and understanding? Let
> him show by his good behavior his deeds in the
> gentleness of wisdom. But if you have bitter
> jealousy and selfish ambition in your heart, do
> not be arrogant and so lie against the truth. This
> wisdom is not that which comes down from
> above, but is earthly, natural, demonic. For where
> jealousy and selfish ambition exist, there is dis-
> order and every evil thing. But the wisdom from
> above is first pure, then peaceable, gentle, rea-
> sonable, full of mercy and good fruits, unwaver-
> ing, without hypocrisy (James 3:13-17).

Remember Satan's basic characteristic, self-centeredness? When jealousy and selfish ambition appear in the
church, we know the source. They signify that demonic
forces are at work in our midst, leading us away from the
wisdom of God. Where these are allowed to flourish
unopposed, spiritual growth, which thrives in an environment of peace, will be stifled.

I've seen enormous amounts of jealousy and selfish
ambition in the church. Until my personal experiences with
demonic oppression, I didn't understand that these things
are a direct result of demonic activity. I thought they were
just the outworkings of people's self-centeredness.

What do you think causes much of the strife in your
church staff? Who causes preachers to become merchandisers of religion rather than ministers of the gospel? Who
stirs in people a desire for power and a resistance to serving
God and others? That's not God! That is Satan doing his

dirty work in our midst. We have built religious kingdoms where real righteousness, based on peace and gentleness, cannot survive.

In Psalm 74 we have an example of the spiritual warfare encountered by the Israelites. It provides us with some insights into our struggle with spirits of jealousy and selfish ambition:

> Turn Thy footsteps toward the perpetual ruins; the enemy has damaged everything within the sanctuary. Thine adversaries have roared in the midst of Thy meeting place; they have set up their own standards for signs (vv. 3-4).

Many people don't want to go to church anymore because they hear the voice of the enemy roaring. He uses human voices to make himself heard.

I sat one day for two hours and listened to a group of preachers engaged in a fierce argument about how to have a soul-winning crusade. Satan was roaring in their midst, and they couldn't agree on anything.

Another of Satan's tactics is to confuse our standards of measuring success. Too often we follow the world's standards. We think bigger is always better. We want to be accepted in the association, win people's approval, have a big budget. Yet the greatest success in my life happened when I lost the crowds and gained the glory of God. Real victory came when I was willing to walk on, knowing that if nobody ever supported me again, God was pleased. That's when I knew the enemy's standards of success had been stripped from my life.

We must embrace God's standards of success. We must

be willing to live sacrificially, to give up everything to help somebody in trouble. Jesus left heaven and gave up His glory to lift us out of defeat, despair and sin. He brought the kingdom of heaven into human lives, and He began to cast out demons, including spirits of jealousy and selfish ambition. As His disciples we can have a part in that ministry of redemption and deliverance.

Truth That Divides

Satan wants to turn us all into Pharisees. If in your defense of the truth you criticize and attack people, you could be under the influence of demonic spirits. If you find yourself saying, "I'm glad I'm not like those other folks," then there's no doubt about the source of your "inspiration." You're living in defeat and being deceived.

Biblical truth will always divide, and that's not necessarily bad. If we examine a passage or a doctrine from several points of view, we can often discover more about what God is trying to say to us. We need the wisdom of the whole body of Christ to understand the whole revelation of God. The devil's trick, though, is to get us arguing about things that are less important than our mutual commitment to Christ. Once our focus slips off Jesus, our slide into Pharisaism begins.

If we are to seek the truth, we must embrace "the gentleness of wisdom" (James 3:13). There is such a need for "gentle wisdom" in the church today. If we live with hatred and bitterness in our hearts, we will be run down by the enemy and dragged off into bondage. The bitterness of the Pharisees will ultimately destroy us.

Beware of justifying pharisaical attitudes by saying you're

"discerning the spirits." If the Holy Spirit gives us the ability to discern spirits, He will also give us the ability to love those who may have been deceived or defeated by them. If we don't have the love, we shouldn't claim to have the discernment.

We even need to learn to love the Pharisees in our midst. We may oppose their teaching and practices, but we are commanded to love them. Jesus never stopped loving the Pharisees. He never said, "Beware of the Pharisees." He said, "Beware of the leaven of the Pharisees." The leaven of the Pharisees is their teaching and influence on people around them. Let us love them and drive out darkness by bringing in light. Let us turn away wrath with a soft answer. Let us overcome the evil influence of the Pharisees with the good influence of Jesus.

We not only need love and forgiveness when we fail, but we also need to offer it to all who fail. I failed miserably. I was totally defeated, and God's grace and love delivered me. We must offer hurting Christians hope. Remember, the prodigal *was a son.*

Misidentifying the Enemy

All of Satan's strategies to attack the church — pride, conflict, jealousy, selfish ambition, idolatry, whatever — share one common component: confusion about the identity of our real enemy. Because people can't see demonic spirits and are often told such spirits don't exist, they think of one another as the enemy. That's exactly what Satan wants us to think.

Those controlled by religious demons have always looked for enemies in the wrong places. The Sadducees, Pharisees and scribes first attacked John the Baptist as their enemy. Then they turned on Jesus and the disciples. In their blind confusion they even labeled Jesus as a demon. Meanwhile, they conspired with King Herod and the Romans to get rid of Him. They were pawns of the real enemy — Satan, who is a murderer.

In one church the pastor's daughter struggled to overcome a drug addiction. The people in the church loved her and tried to help her, but without much success. Later she discovered she was pregnant out of wedlock. The congregation loved her, forgave her and tried to help her raise her baby.

Then someone invited this troubled young woman to a prayer meeting. At that meeting there were people who believed in deliverance and believed God could set her free. She was delivered from the deep hurt in her heart — the root cause of her other problems — and freed from her addictions to drugs and sex. When her church found out what had happened, they refused to have anything further to do with her. They kicked her out of her father's church!

A few weeks later she showed up at one of their services, walked to the front and said, "I took drugs, and you loved me. I got pregnant, and you loved me. I went to a prayer meeting and got set free, and now you won't speak to me."

The people in her church considered the prayer group a threat to their doctrinal purity. While they were busy separating themselves from "false doctrine," the real enemy sowed the seeds of hatred and bondage in their midst.

Don't let yourself be fooled. Our real enemy is not a theological group or movement. Our enemy is the power of darkness that strikes at us all, making one doubt the Bible and another act like a Pharisee. Our real enemy is Satan and his demonic hosts. They are running unobserved and unopposed through much of the body of Christ. It is time we learned how to stop them.

Summary

Satan follows certain identifiable patterns in attacking the church. He may induce people to worship their church or denomination rather than God. Often he puffs people up with theological pride, convincing them they are superior to others because of what they believe. He can also use particular biblical truths to incite conflict among believers. All of his strategies for attacking the church display one common element: They try to confuse believers concerning the true identity of the enemy and get them fighting against one another.

FOUR

SATAN ATTACKS FAMILIES

SOME APPALLING TRENDS ARE occurring today. Families are filled with despair and defeat; separation and divorce are the order of the day, while those who remain married often have an existence rather than a life. Yet God could not have given man a greater companion than woman, nor could He have created a better friend for woman than man. So why do so few seem to enjoy the beautiful family relationships God intended? Simple. Someone is destroying those relationships.

A force is leveled against the family, and it is most effective in robbing us of the joy God intends us to have. That force will continue to succeed until we open our eyes to what is really happening in our families. What we label just plain meanness or incompatibility is often demonic activity.

A husband gnashes his teeth at his wife in uncontrollable anger. A wife nags incessantly, taunts or criticizes her husband. Or the two seem utterly unable to communicate. Children snarl and behave like untamed animals. They rebel and react to parental correction with irrational hostility or stubbornness. Parents obstinately refuse to listen to the hurts and problems of their children when it's obvious their insensitivity is destroying the parent-child relationship.

People seek advice and solutions from psychologists and secular counselors, but often these are not problems the wisdom of men can solve — they are expressions of the personalities of demons! The forces of darkness have invaded our families, and their agents are in control, producing "disorder and every evil thing." The problems are being caused by supernatural, spiritual powers, and they will not yield to anything less than the greater supernatural, spiritual power of the kingdom of God.

There is only one answer to the strife that plagues Christian marriages and families today: "You are from God, little children, and have overcome them; because greater is He who is in you than he who is in the world" (1 John 4:4). By relying on the remedies of men, much of the church is playing into the hands of the enemy.

My wife, Betty, and I were reading mail from our television viewers when she said to me tearfully, "I don't think I can stand reading anymore. It seems that when men get to be about forty years old, they leave their wives and kids and run off with younger women. What's going on?"

What's going on is that many people, by loving themselves, are being snared by the enemy. It is Satan who makes men spurn the wives who have borne their children. It's the devil who prompts a wife and mother to run away with her boss, leaving behind a shocked and hurting family. It's Satan who leads a generation of youngsters down the path to destruction.

Recruiting Kids for the Occult

We watch, horrified, as our kids are trapped by things we never taught them how to resist. It's time we wake up: Satan wants to lure our children into the world's meaningless forms of happiness. He wants to ensnare them in the pursuit of pleasure, robbing them of the innocence and joy that could be theirs in Christ.

Satan has trapped many of the youth of America through the enticement of drugs. Peer pressure, the desire to be accepted, and the brief rush caused by a drug-induced high are destroying millions of young lives. Hard-rock music with godless and suggestive lyrics has not only brainwashed youth but has used sensual suggestions to make teens vulnerable. They become intoxicated by the beat and move in concert with demonic impressions.

Sex has always been the chief attraction to teens and the poorest possible substitute for true love. Now with the family unit weakened, young people are giving themselves to one another with no accountability or responsibility.

But not only drugs, sex and rock music threaten these youngsters; the devil would have them sell their souls through satanism and witchcraft. Listen to what Jerry Johnston, author of *The Edge of Evil: The Rise of Satanism in North America,* has to say about this:

> Kids started coming to my assemblies dressed in black, wearing black nail polish, black eye makeup, and graffiti such as "Live" (evil spelled backwards) and "Natas" (Satan spelled backwards). We went to cities where we encountered young people who were demon-possessed. In St. Louis, I stood with a police officer and a paramedic and a girl's parents. She weighed 95 pounds and four men were holding her to the ground growling like a dog. I knew then that something needed to be said. So we carried out a year-long investigation resulting in the book....
>
> When we met with a member of the Chicago police department's gang crime unit, he reminded us that there are four distinct levels of satanic activity in America now. Category one is the teen-age dabbler. Category two is the self-styled satanist, these autonomous, covert groups that blend so inconspicuously into a city, yet according to the FBI they are in every major vocation....The third category is the religious public satanists. Category four is the hard core satanic cults. We investigated human sacrifice.[1]

Jerry Johnston goes on to describe how our culture

inundates children with satanic messages and paranormal activity. He points out that movies constantly promote this area, from films such as *Ghostbusters* which emphasize the paranormal, to movies like the *Omen* trilogy which blatantly portray evil. He also discusses heavy metal rock music that has lyrics about demonic ceremonies and human sacrifice. Young teens especially are vulnerable to seduction by witches and satanists. Jerry Johnston says:

> We've found repeatedly that kids are invited to parties, they get drunk or stoned, then...are invited to a select private room where they are photographed or videotaped in a sexually compromising situation, sometimes orgy, group sex. Concurrently, they are introduced to a contract, a covenant with Satan. They're asked to draw or drink blood....This seems to be part of the theatrics. Later they try to renege and their life or their family's lives are threatened. That's why teenage satanists commonly feel that they cannot get out once they get in.[2]

Listen to the story of one teenager, Sean Sellers, who was deceived by Satan in this way:

> When I was about 10 years old, I had a baby-sitter who introduced me to the occult in the form of some books. At 13 I got involved with Dungeons and Dragons. It became an obsession. Then at 15 I got introduced to a witch and she took me on as her disciple...and got me involved in satanism. She had a piece of human skin from when she was

witness to a human sacrifice. Her first words to me were, "Well, you can go white magic or you can go black magic. White magic is kind of hypocritical, but if you want power, you go black magic." And so I said, "OK, let's go black magic." And she said, "The first thing you have to do is pray to Satan."

I got caught drinking blood in my history class one day and that drew a lot of attention to me. Then I got caught with my satanic bible at school and that really drew a lot of attention. When I first started learning rituals, I began with pentagram and magic circles and different talismans in order to keep demons away. As I got more into this philosophy of good and evil being interchanged, I began to think of demons as my friends and I began to see that I was mistreating them by doing this, so I began to invoke demons and ask them to enter my body. I would say, "This is a sanctuary for you, please come in." They would....

In satanism there comes a point where you have to give [Satan] everything. So we began to prove our allegiance to Satan by breaking God's commandments. In the end there was only one that remained unbroken: "You shall not murder"....[3]

Eventually Sean and a friend killed a convenience-store clerk. Then, after a recurring dream about killing his parents "in the name of Satan," Sean turned the dream into reality. He was convicted of his parents' murder and sentenced to prison. Someone slipped a Bible through the bars of his cell. Right there in the cell Sean went through a deliverance and received Jesus as his Savior.

I talked about this subject with Michael Haynes, Ph.D., a former Baptist pastor who has become an expert on the occult and satanic crimes. He warns: "Kids are the target because they make easy victims. [Those in the occult] always prey upon people who are very creative, who are of high intelligence and low self-esteem or low achievement."[4] He said the occult has three major areas for recruitment: college campuses, the military and day-care centers.

I asked Dr. Haynes what he would recommend a person do if he or she knew a child was involved in the occult. Here's what he said:

> If you know a child is involved in this, tell somebody. Tell his parents. A lot of times that doesn't work, but at least you've done something. Then move into battle for that child on your knees. This is a spiritual battleground. What has actually arrested this person's mind has come through the spiritual dimension into the physical expression of a book or a magazine or a tape or music or something that's captured their attention. When the thief comes, he comes to steal, kill and destroy. The way he steals is very subtle. He simply gets their attention.
>
> Then you begin to really show care and wade through some pretty heavy stuff. Love is the most powerful force on the earth. You don't reject them because of what they're doing and who they are. You love them like our Lord loved them. He walked among them with power. Jesus lives inside

59

us, and we're just ignorant of the power that's in us.

I don't think that experts *per se* are the people who need to come in and deal with this issue. We all are the body of Christ, and we all should be able to deal with this issue.[5]

Anyone who doesn't believe Satan is a murderer is deceived. His intent is murder. He not only wants to destroy physical life; he also wants to steal our joy of living, to make us, in effect, zombies. He wants us numb to reality. Let's learn to be overcomers — how to have the victory through Jesus Christ.

Summary

Since the family is used by God, perhaps even more so than the church, as an instrument for teaching people about Jesus and the Christian walk, Satan reserves some of his most vicious attacks for the family. He attacks all family relationships by sending demons to distort and disrupt communication between husband and wife, parents and children. Our kids are among Satan's choice targets. With sex, drugs, alcohol and peer pressure, he lures them into paths of destruction. In recent years this path increasingly has led to the occult and Satan worship — the ultimate devastation. To combat these attacks, Christian adults — particularly parents — must be alert to Satan's work and go to the rescue of any youngster who shows signs of occult involvement.

FIVE

SATAN ATTACKS INDIVIDUAL CHRISTIANS

HERE I WAS, A CHRISTIAN, YET I was living in recurring defeat. I couldn't stop overeating. My temper flared. I was often rude. The words of my Bible would bore into me: "the fruit of the Spirit is kindness." Why then was I so unkind to people, even people in my family?

61

Something was wrong. A preacher shouldn't behave this way. I couldn't control my thought life. Eventually I convinced myself it wasn't possible for a normal man to live without lust, to conquer it.

At the outset of my Christian pilgrimage I loved the Word of God and could hardly wait to read it. Then it became a tool of my trade, a sermon book. That first, sweet love was gone. I had been deceived. I had become a prisoner.

Sadly, many believers live as prisoners — and they think this is the normal way to live! They are unable to share their faith. Their Bibles collect dust or are toted around in leather bindings only to impress others.

A very personal battle is taking place.

The Scriptures warn that we can be held captive. First Corinthians 10:11 explains that the experiences of Israel are given to us as examples of spiritual reality. The ancient Hebrews didn't believe their enemies could invade the promised land and take them captive. Yet Israel was overrun again and again. Most of the Old Testament chronicles the story of God's people living as prisoners in the promised land.

Learn from the Israelites: Don't be deceived into believing you can't be attacked by the enemy, that demonic beings can't really bother you. Who do you think is driving the life of God out of your church? Who do you think is filling people in the church with animosity, skepticism and unbelief? Who do you think is causing people to resist, criticize and judge each other? The fact that these things are happening is visible evidence that the kingdom of darkness is influencing believers.

God described Israel's enemies as "your tormentors, who have said to you, 'Lie down that we may walk over you.'

You have even made your back like the ground...for those who walk over it" (Is. 51:23). That's what the devil has done to many of us. He said, "Lie down!" We obeyed, and he just ran over us like a bulldozer. None of us has to put up with that! But some of us do. I did!

Please understand: I am not talking about Christians being possessed by demons. We Christians are not powerless; we can't lay all the blame for our actions at the feet of demons. Christians cannot be possessed. Christians can, however, be assaulted and oppressed by the devil.

How does this happen? Simple: We give ground to Satan. It's like giving up part of your property. Other people don't own the land, but if you let them use it and build on it, they'll take over. Likewise, if you allow the enemy to move into your home and take over areas of your life, he'll build a stronghold — brick by brick — and do things to harm you and your family.

Consider David. The Bible calls him a man after God's own heart, yet lust overcame him. He did not walk in the will of God, nor abide in the Word. In a day when kings went out to war, David stayed home and let others fight the battles. Rather than routing the enemy, he was taking a stroll on the balcony.

How many Christians who have been called as soldiers of the Lord Jesus, who are more than conquerors in His name, have chosen not to go to war against the powers of darkness? They do not put on the whole armor of God. They stroll on the balcony — and even pick up binoculars so they can zero in on the enticements of the world. As surely as David fell and succumbed to sin, so do they.

We Rebel Against God

One way we believers are defeated is when we rebel against God; He often turns us over to the enemy for judgment. Jesus warned us about this in Matthew 18 when He told the parable of the unforgiving slave. This man, who had been forgiven a great debt by his lord, refused to forgive his fellow slave a very small debt.

When the lord found out about the slave's actions, he said, "You wicked slave, I forgave you all that debt because you entreated me. Should you not also have had mercy on your fellow slave?" Jesus finished the story by saying, "And his lord, moved with anger, handed him over to the torturers until he should repay all that was owed him. So shall My heavenly Father also do to you, if each of you does not forgive his brother from your heart" (Matt. 18:32-35).

If we refuse the heart and mind of Christ, which says, "I forgive," we are in direct disobedience to God. And Jesus says if we refuse to forgive, God will turn us over to "the torturers."

Most people are tortured in their minds. They can't forget what somebody did to them. They seem incapable of forgiving, but the fact is they choose not to forgive. Through this resistance the enemy gets a stranglehold on them — they are tormented.

Paul also warned us about God's judgment through the enemy. After explaining about the freedom we have in Christ, he wrote, "Take heed therefore, so that the thing spoken of in the Prophets may not come upon you: 'Behold, you scoffers, and marvel, and perish; for I am accomplishing a work in your days, a work which you will never believe, though someone should describe it to you' " (Acts

13:40-41).

Paul would not warn us about something that couldn't possibly happen. Rather, he says, "take heed...so that the thing spoken of in the Prophets may not come upon you." What is the thing spoken of in the Prophets? Paul was quoting from Habakkuk 1:5-6, where God says, "I am doing something in your days — you would not believe if you were told. For behold, I am raising up the Chaldeans, that fierce and impetuous people who march throughout the earth to seize dwelling places which are not theirs." The Chaldeans were the enemy, and God was raising them up against His own people.

God used the enemy to bring judgment against His people. "Thou, O Lord, hast appointed them to judge; and Thou, O Rock, hast established them to correct," we read in Habakkuk 1:12. The rest of the book of Habakkuk records how God's people rebelled against Him. God kept His word; He used the enemy to judge them — and He'll do the same to us.

God uses the devil as the rod of His correction, to bring judgment and even destruction to those who refuse to live in the shadow of the Almighty. If you're not holding on to Jesus, you are vulnerable to the power of the enemy, and he will defeat you.

The prophet Habakkuk described how the enemy works: "Why hast Thou made men like the fish of the sea, like creeping things without a ruler over them? The Chaldeans bring all of them up with a hook, drag them away with their net, and gather them together in their fishing net" (Hab. 1:14-15). The enemy hooked God's people; they got ensnared.

So it is in the lives of far too many Christians. The enemy

65

comes in and hooks them, whether it's on alcohol, drugs, food, sex, money, power or some other pleasure. The only way to withstand the assault of the devil is to walk in faithfulness to the Lord and to the Word.

The Bible says in 1 Corinthians 3:9 that we are God's cultivated field. If you abandon a cultivated field, it grows weeds and briars like no other field. Likewise, a Christian who resists God will grow the weeds and briars of enemy activity and face a chaos that not only is indescribable but unbearable.

Most of us think our problems are simply the result of bad habits in our lives. Don't believe it! Someone is hooking us, enticing us, ultimately controlling us. You say, "But, James, the devil can't do anything against my will." True, but you may unwittingly submit your will to him.

The moment your will is not totally committed to the will of God, Satan has a hook in you. The moment you turn away from God; the moment you cease to love Him with all your heart, soul, mind and strength; the moment you stop living by the Word, Satan has his claws in you. Then he can deceive and mislead you.

Satan Deceives Us

Many Christians are controlled by some habit or addiction. They are in bondage. But Satan blinds them, making them think they are following Christ even though their behavior is ruled by this habit. They say they are filled with the Spirit while they are actually stuffing themselves with food. They boast that they don't drink. The truth is they couldn't drink if they wanted to, because their stomachs are already so full of food. They don't recognize that gluttony is as much a sin as drunkenness.

Some gossip about brothers and sisters who have fallen into "gross sins." Instead they should minister to them in love and forgiveness, realizing that every sin is gross in God's eyes — especially their own self-righteousness.

Paul talked about deceiving spirits when he wrote to Timothy: "But the Spirit explicitly says that in later times some will fall away from the faith, paying attention to deceitful spirits and doctrines of demons, by means of the hypocrisy of liars seared in their own conscience as with a branding iron" (1 Tim. 4:1-2).

Jesus said if you don't receive the Word gladly, then what you have received will be taken away. He said to be careful what you hear, because what you hear — and think and see — determines what you are. Choose carefully the things you listen to, the things you think, the things you set before your eyes. Be on the alert.

Unforgiving Spirits of Bitterness

Bitter believers are a common sight in the church, and the enemy has come in to torment them. They weren't alert; they didn't see the devil stalking them. All they saw was someone — some flesh-and-blood person — who offended them. That person, the "offender," was wrong, as wrong as the people who spit on Jesus and drove the spikes in His hands. Yet Jesus said, "Father, forgive them."

You will always find people in the church who offend you. Sometimes they live in your home. Naturally you become resentful — and thus open the door to the spirit of bitterness. Did you know that every time you withdraw from fellowship with the rest of the body, you become vulnerable to the devil? And when you cut others off from your fellowship, you make them vulnerable. When we cut ourselves off from one another, everybody suffers. Well, not everybody. The devil and his demons celebrate.

This is illustrated in Paul's letters to the Corinthian church. There was a man in the church who had committed gross immorality. Paul said, "I have decided to deliver such a one to Satan for the destruction of his flesh, that his spirit may be saved in the day of the Lord Jesus" (1 Cor. 5:5). Paul cut off fellowship from the man.

In 2 Corinthians Paul wrote about the same person:

> Sufficient for such a one is this punishment which was inflicted by the majority, so that on the contrary you should rather forgive and comfort him, lest somehow such a one be overwhelmed by excessive sorrow. Wherefore I urge you to reaffirm your love for him....But whom you forgive anything, I forgive also...for your sakes in the presence of Christ, in order that no advantage be taken of us by Satan; for we are not ignorant of his schemes (vv. 2:6-8,10-11).

Paul commended them for dealing with the moral problem, but he also commended their forgiveness. Paul himself forgave the man so that Satan couldn't take advantage of the situation.

If you treat a brother or sister in Christ harshly, you are vulnerable to the enemy. I'm not talking about situations in which you confront evil. But when you confront sin, you've got to forgive. No matter what. If you allow resentment to fester in your heart, the tormenters are sure to follow.

Condemning Spirits

Another spirit the devil sends is the spirit of condemnation. When we feel condemned, we become discouraged. And discouragement is one of the greatest enemies any of us can face, for it usually leads to despair, to giving up — which is a step toward destruction.

Don't you think when Peter got up to preach at Pentecost the enemy reminded him of how he had denied Christ three times? How could Peter preach about this wonderful, matchless grace, knowing that he had denied Christ, that the enemy had been able to "sift" him (Luke 22:31)?

Peter overcame any condemning spirits with the truth: Jesus had forgiven him and instructed him to strengthen the brothers and tend His sheep (Luke 22:32; John 21:15-17). Like Peter, we must not let Satan condemn us and convince us to give up. The road to victory lies in confession of our sins and acceptance of Christ's forgiveness.

Sickness Attacks Us

The enemy also attacks us through sickness — spirits of infirmity. Almost every believer today thinks it's normal to be sick. I believe it's normal for sickness to attack us and for us to fight back in response. We live in a fallen world, but so did Jesus, and He wasn't sick. God's provision is divine health.

Don't get down on yourself or hide when you're sick. Instead, call for help and say, "Let's pray." It's true that some sickness is caused by the diseased environment of this world. It's also true that the enemy will afflict us in any way he can. He may be the cause of some of the sickness we face.

Look at this example from Jesus' ministry: "And He was teaching in one of the synagogues on the Sabbath. And behold, there was a woman who for eighteen years had had a sickness caused by a spirit; and she was bent double, and could not straighten up at all" (Luke 13:10-11). Here was a sickness caused by a spirit. Jesus called this woman a daughter of Abraham, a daughter of the promise (v. 16). She was a child of God, yet she was bound by a spirit. Likewise, it's possible for Christians to have their bodies attacked by evil spirits of infirmity.

Many of us get sicknesses because we've never learned to resist them with God's help. God wants us to fight back against sickness. There are spirits of disease and sickness, and we leave ourselves wide open to them anytime we are passive and forget to resist the enemy.

People who have a passive spirit or personality are the most likely candidates for cancer. Those who keep everything inside are also good candidates for cancer and heart disease. Angry people are at risk as well. Unconfessed and uncontrolled anger gives the enemy a prime opportunity to tear your whole body apart. Remember, Satan is a destroyer. Don't be surprised that he tries to destroy your health along with everything else.

You may say, "Some of the sweetest people I know are sick." Maybe all they ever learned how to be was sweet. They never learned how to resist the enemy. Nobody ever told them to fight; nobody ever told them a thief was coming to steal their health.

Spirits of Fear

God does not give His children a spirit of fear (2 Tim. 1:7), but there are spirits of fear ruling the lives of many Christians. My wife was delivered from a spirit of fear that had hindered her much of her life. It made her feel unworthy to be my wife. There was a time when she thought she was going to die because she was not a fit companion for a well-known evangelist.

She wasn't a gifted musician, singer or teacher. "I don't have any talent," Betty often commented.

Satan had blinded her to the inner beauty and qualities that made her a wonderful wife and mother. Nothing I said seemed to help. God gloriously delivered her from fear shortly after my own deliverance.

Whenever we believe Satan's lies, we suffer the consequences through the deterioration of our character — the beauty of Jesus in us begins to erode. If the process goes on long enough, Satan will establish a stronghold of fear, deceit and corruption in our lives. We may simply get used to his influence co-existing with that of Jesus.

This critical stage requires help from other parts of the body of Christ. We must humble ourselves before God and seek out other Christians if we want deliverance and healing. We need their insights, love and prayers to win victory over these strongholds. We need the power of God's gentle wisdom to defeat the long-established lies of the enemy. Remember: Free people can free people!

Summary

As individuals, believers expose themselves to satanic

attack by rebelling against God. Satan also may keep believers in bondage by blinding them to captivity. He sometimes sends unforgiving spirits upon Christians, causing them to become isolated from the strengthening fellowship of other believers. He attacks through physical sickness and through spirits of fear. When an enemy attack comes, we must humble ourselves before God and seek the help of other believers. This is the primary provision God has made for setting us free.

SIX

THE NATURE
OF STRONGHOLDS

No ASPECT OF SPIRITUAL WARFARE IS
more important than the destruction of strongholds in our
lives. As long as they remain entrenched, we will live in
recurring defeat.

Most teaching on strongholds is based on Paul's words
to the church at Corinth:

> For though we live in the world, we do not wage war as the world does. The weapons we fight with are not the weapons of the world....they have divine power to demolish strongholds....arguments and every pretension that sets itself up against the knowledge of God, and we take captive every thought to make it obedient to Christ (2 Cor. 10:3-5, NIV).

What are these strongholds, and what are the weapons of divine power we can use to demolish them? To find out, let's review the biblical view of human nature. Because we are created in the image of the triune God, we are made up of three parts: spirit, soul and body. The spirit is our nature, what we are. The soul is our personality, how we think, feel and behave. The body, of course, is the physical container for the spirit and soul.

In speaking of strongholds, Paul refers to "every thought," "pretensions" and "arguments." Clearly all these things are associated with how we think, feel and behave. They come from the mind and soul, rather than from the spirit or the body.

It is important to understand this because the New Testament teaches that a Christian's spirit is inhabited by the Spirit of God and does not produce sin (2 Pet. 1:4). John said, "No one who is born of God practices sin, because His seed abides in him; and he cannot sin, because he is born of God" (1 John 3:9). Never make the mistake of saying that Satan's strongholds can overthrow the Spirit of God in believers. Satan and his demons are no match for the Spirit of God when we are submitted to His lordship.

Yet the Bible makes it quite clear that a Christian can sin.

As Paul says in Romans 7:23, this behavior originates from "sin which is in my members." Because we know sin does not originate in the believer's spirit (2 Pet. 1:4), the "members" to which Paul refers must be the soul and body. Paul says there is a "law of sin" that operates through these members, producing sinful behavior. The word "law," as used here, refers to a principle, like the law of gravity. It is not a written code. Paul is identifying a force or principle that operates in both the soul and the body. It encourages us to ignore the influence of our reborn spirit, which is one with Christ.

Thus, the strongholds Paul speaks of in 2 Corinthians 10 are patterns of thinking and feeling. These patterns are instruments of the law of sin operating through our body and soul.

The law of sin and its operations are part of our former sin nature, the "old man" inherited from Adam and crucified with Christ on the cross. The rebellion and self-centeredness of these patterns of thought and behavior leave us exposed to demonic influence. Since this exposure begins at birth, Satan exercises extensive influence over the development of our body and soul. No wonder he is so successful at building strongholds in us.

In Ephesians 2 Paul describes our condition before we came to Christ:

> And you were dead in your...sins, in which you formerly walked according to the course of this world, according to the prince of the power of the air....Among them we too all formerly lived in the lusts of our flesh, indulging the desires of the flesh and of the mind, and were by nature children

of wrath, even as the rest" (vv. 1-3).

Strongholds are the patterns that were built up in us while we were still "slaves of sin" (Rom. 6:17). In the revolutionary spiritual change that occurs when a believer becomes a new creation in Christ (2 Cor. 5:17), many of these satanic patterns are obliterated. Some strongholds, however, may still stand — and those are the strongholds to which Paul refers in 2 Corinthians 10. Satan and his demonic cohorts work to reinforce strongholds that are weakened as the Holy Spirit reproduces the character of Jesus in our lives. The enemy can create diversions to keep us from using our spiritual authority and weapons to destroy them.

When we fail to destroy strongholds, we allow some measure of demonic influence to remain in our lives. The stronghold of rebellion, for example, is associated with witchcraft (1 Sam. 15:23). Jealousy and selfish ambition are described as demonic (James 3:14-15).

As Christians we must confront strongholds, seeking the discernment of the Holy Spirit to recognize and cast out any demons that are present. But be prepared to see some kind of demonic activity.

Unfortunately, some Christians take the issue of demonic influence through strongholds too far. They believe the strongholds themselves are demons residing in or possessing them. Scripture contains nothing to support that doctrine. If we accept it, we will battle Satan in ignorance and risk tragic defeat. What we fight against are demons taking advantage of strongholds in our lives. The strongholds are not demons. If they were, we could use our authority from God to cast out the demons and permanently eliminate the problem. In practice, we find that these problems often return. This is because we are fighting a stronghold, not just a demon. Our faith will be undermined unless we understand what we are tangling with. Anytime a Christian gives ground to Satan through unbelief or disobedience, the enemy will establish or strengthen the stronghold.

Examples of Strongholds

Paul listed some examples of strongholds in Ephesians 4:22-32, where he urged believers to "lay aside" the things that pertained to the "old self." These include lying, stealing, corrupt communication, bitterness, wrath, anger, clamor, slander and malice. The old, self-centered nature wanted everything to go its way. When things didn't cooperate, it was frustrated, producing hostility. Everything in Paul's list is an expression of hostility directed either internally or toward others.

We should suspect that a stronghold exists when we see recurring hostile thoughts, feelings or behavior patterns. If you use deceit, intimidation and manipulation to get your way, you are controlled by strongholds. Likewise if you are in the habit of either lashing out or seething in silence whenever you're frustrated. Hostility turned inward may produce physical illness or lead to substance abuse — further evidence that strongholds will destroy our very lives.

Characteristics of Strongholds

Always remember that strongholds are the work of Satan. They are serious business. Jesus said the devil has come

77

only to steal, kill and destroy (John 10:10). Satan's strongholds can steal our joy and peace, kill our relationships with others and destroy our opportunities for enjoying the abundant life in Christ. When unconfronted, strongholds make slaves of us.

This was the experience of God's people in the Old Testament. Nehemiah 9 summarizes the story of God's mercy and Israel's disobedience. The Israelites allowed strongholds of idolatry, greed and fear to develop in the land God had given them. Their hostility drove them to kill the prophets God sent them (v. 26). In the end, as they surveyed the ruins of Jerusalem, this is what they had to say:

> "However, Thou art just in all that has come upon us; for Thou hast dealt faithfully, but we have acted wickedly. For [we]...have not kept Thy law or paid attention to Thy commandments and Thine admonitions....But they...did not serve Thee or turn from their evil deeds. Behold, we are slaves today, and as to the land which Thou didst give to our fathers to eat of its fruit and its bounty, behold, we are slaves on it" (vv. 33-36).

The people of Israel had allowed enemies to distract them from their God. Strongholds of evil had grown up around them. Now they were prisoners in the promised land. Unless we learn to tear down strongholds, we will share their fate. Many Christians, even Spirit-filled Christians, are living in defeat.

When you joke or even boast about a stronghold — "my temper," "my greed," "my disorderliness" — you are playing into Satan's hands. The last thing he wants is for you to uncover the sinister nature of these "personality traits" and turn to God for their destruction.

How do you recognize strongholds? While individual strongholds can differ greatly from each other, certain characteristics about them remain constant.

Strongholds are stubborn. They seem impossible to topple. Strongholds cannot be torn down through religious activity. If we attack them in our own strength, they may appear to weaken or vanish temporarily, only to reappear — sometimes stronger than before. After years of trying to get rid of them, people often give up and simply "learn to live with them."

Strongholds are irrational. They don't make sense. Their influence on you will defy logic. Smoking is an obvious example of this characteristic. It's a messy, offensive habit that leaves you with foul-smelling breath and clothing. It's expensive, and it causes your skin to wrinkle at an early age. According to medical research, it ruins your health and shortens your life. Yet millions of people continue to puff cigarettes. That defies logic.

Strongholds are uncontrollable. If you pinpoint a habit or behavior pattern that seems to control you, you have discovered a stronghold in your life. It may be your temper or feelings of depression. You may have trouble telling the truth or keeping confidences. You may eat too much or too little. Whatever it is, you can't stop it. No matter how firmly you resolve to resist a stronghold, it always gets the better of you.

Strongholds are counterproductive. A stronghold will appear to be helpful, while it is actually destroying us. The abuse of drugs and alcohol are classic examples of this. Turning to these chemical means of escape only leads to a captivity much more cruel and powerful than the problems we were trying to avoid.

Strongholds always fail you. The "strategies" Satan has given us to cope with life's frustrations only bring more frustration. Instead of solving problems, they make life worse.

Design of a Stronghold

By carefully examining Paul's advice in 2 Corinthians 10, we can learn how to overcome strongholds both in our own lives and in the lives of others. However, to confront strongholds successfully we must study their design as thoroughly as a general would study the layout of an enemy fortification before attacking.

A Christian counselor discovered the truth of this when he was meeting with a woman who had an obsessive fear of harming her children. Over a period of weeks they prayed for God's power to overcome this stronghold, but they experienced no success. Then before one session they prayed for God to identify and remove the barriers to victory. That prayer was answered.

The stronghold, as it turned out, was not a single struc-ture. Instead, it resembled the Alamo in Texas, a fort standing within protective walls. The stronghold had three basic elements, all mentioned by Paul in 2 Corinthians 10:

The stronghold itself. The center of any stronghold com-plex is a fortified prison or dungeon within which unhealthy patterns of thought and feeling can hold us captive. With God's supernatural firepower, such prisons can be leveled, freeing us to follow Christ. The counselor discovered that in the woman's case this central fortress was her fear.

The inner wall ("arguments"). As she talked about her problem, the woman said, "I don't know why I can't figure this thing out. I've tried to make sense of it, but the more I think about it, the more confused I become." At that moment the Lord showed the counselor the significance of the word "arguments" (2 Cor. 10:5, NIV) — translated as "reasonings," "imaginations," "speculations" and "rationalizations." The stronghold's inner prison of fear still stood because the woman was attacking it through her own reflection and analysis. Her dependence on human intellect had become a wall surrounding the inner prison and protecting it from attack.

Intellectual and psychological weapons are ineffective when used against strongholds. The enemy establishes strongholds with supernatural, spiritual power, and we have to use supernatural, spiritual power from God to break them down.

The counselor stressed that the woman would have to rely on the supernatural power of God to overcome the stronghold. She would have to "demolish arguments" and set aside her insistence on understanding everything involved in her deliverance. It would take childlike trust in God, not human understanding (Prov. 3:5-6).

An outer wall ("every pretension"). Later in the session the woman said one of her fears was that her Christian friends would discover her problem and doubt her credibility as a disciple. "They all think I'm a strong Christian," she said.

"Why does it bother you that they might discover you have problems?" the counselor asked. "Doesn't the Bible say we are to bear one another's burdens?"

"Oh, I guess it's just pride," she answered.

As she said this, the Holy Spirit pointed the counselor to this third element in the design of a stronghold: "every pretension that sets itself up against the knowledge of God" (v. 5, NIV).

Suddenly it was clear. A second wall surrounded the inner wall and protected the entire stronghold: the wall of pride. The word "pretension" is also translated "lofty thing" and "proud thing." Considering Paul's military analogy throughout this passage, we should picture a high, defensive wall. Such a structure always looks proud and defiant. In this case it is designed to resist the knowledge of God.

Both the woman and her counselor saw that this great wall of pride would have to be shattered before the stronghold of fear could be destroyed. The woman had to be willing to face embarrassment, ridicule or humiliation — whatever God required — if she was going to find healing and deliverance.

Our prayers can weaken the enemy's grip and give us understanding of one another's problems. But deliverance comes only when we submit to the deliverer — Jesus.

A Strategy for Attack

As this woman's experience shows, we must battle against human pride and human wisdom to penetrate the multilayered defenses of a stronghold. We also need to identify the specific behavior patterns that are keeping us in bondage. But first comes the battle for the mind. Satan relies heavily on deception to cheat us of our birthright of victory in Jesus. Only as our minds are transformed can we hope to overcome such deception (Rom. 12:1-3).

82

With our focus centered on Jesus, we will maintain spiritual health and resistance to satanic attacks. Psalm 18 is a testimony of God's power to deliver us from enemy strongholds:

> "I love Thee, O Lord, my strength." The Lord is my rock and my fortress and my deliverer, my God, my rock, in whom I take refuge; my shield and the horn of my salvation, my stronghold. I call upon the Lord, who is worthy to be praised, and I am saved from my enemies (vv. 1-3).

God has not left us defenseless against the forces of darkness. The weapons of spiritual warfare that He has given us are described in the book of Ephesians. Once we understand these weapons, also called the armor of God, we are ready to enter the battle.

Summary

Satan can control and defeat us through strongholds. These strongholds, as identified by Paul in 2 Corinthians 10:3-5, are structured in the mind. They are the patterns of thought and behavior we have acquired as a result of growing up in a world constantly under attack from demonic principalities and powers. Strongholds often consist of a central fortress and protective outer walls. To overcome a stronghold we must first attack the outer walls — such as pride and self-sufficiency — and then zero in on the main fortress. The power in which we attack, of course, is the almighty power of God, and our weapons are provided by Him.

SEVEN

THE BATTLE FOR
THE MIND

I KNOW I'VE SAID THIS BEFORE, BUT
it can't be overstated: Satan and evil spirits cannot bring
ongoing destructive forces into our lives unless they first
deceive us. This has been true since Adam and Eve. While
they were in the Garden of Eden, Satan could not harm
them. Then he deceived Eve, and we're still suffering from

the results of that deception.

There is a spiritual battle raging for our minds. Whom are we going to believe? The enemy works in an atmosphere of controversy and turmoil. When we listen to him, we get worried, confused, full of strife and doubt. We become vulnerable to his suggestions. But if we believe that Jesus is our peace, we can express the kingdom of God anywhere. We can have victory over our enemy.

How Satan Attacks the Mind

When we allow Satan to deceive us, we wind up in bondage. For example, some of us have accepted Satan's lie that he doesn't exist or that he can't bother us because we're Christians. He binds us in defeat, discouragement and despair, but we think we're free because we've believed his lies.

We're like the people in John 8 to whom Jesus said, "You shall know the truth, and the truth shall make you free." They said, "We are Abraham's offspring, and have never yet been enslaved to anyone; how is it that You say, 'You shall become free'?" (vv. 32-33).

What an outrageous statement! The Jews were everybody's slave, from the Chaldeans to the Babylonians. At the very time they claimed they weren't slaves, they were slaves of the Roman empire. Talk about being deceived!

Another of Satan's major strategies is to keep God's people ignorant of their ability to combat him and his demons. Some Christians believe in the devil and know he can cause them problems, but they are never taught what to do about it. Some go through life trampled by the enemy, believing it's God's will for them to be crushed by hardship

86

and adversity.

Of course, God can teach us much in our battle with the enemy, and He can fulfill some purpose for our lives in every attack He allows the enemy to bring against us. But it is not God's will for Christians to be ground into the dust by Satan. He has given us the victory through Christ Jesus, and He intends for the victory to be visible so it will draw onlookers to Christ.

Listen to Matthew 5:16: " 'Let your light shine before men in such a way that they may see your good works, and glorify your Father who is in heaven.' "

Other Christians know how to fight the battle, but the enemy has convinced them he is so powerful they can't possibly win. It is true we can never resist and overcome Satan in our own strength, but that's only part of the story. Jesus has given us authority over demons; in Him we are more than conquerors. How tragic that most Christians have less belief in their authority over demons than the demons themselves do. James 2:19 says the devils believe and tremble.

Whatever strategy Satan uses, the battle begins in the mind. My associate Dudley Hall told me about a man who said, "Nobody loves me." On the surface it seemed to be true. His wife and kids had left him; his friends were not talking to him. But he had believed a lie from Satan. The truth is that God loves him and Dudley loves him. But the man can't see beyond the lie that nobody loves him. Dudley said to me, "Until he believes the truth, he'll never be free, and he'll never get rid of that stronghold of rejection."

Here's how the process works: First Satan sows seeds of accusation in our minds. "It's you doing this," he'll say. "You're the bad guy. Why would anybody love you? If you were a better person they might. But you're a loser." As we choose to listen to these lies, we feel condemned. We think our problems are entirely our fault, and we don't recognize the enemy's hand in it. We don't expose him as the liar and accuser that he is.

There are thousands of women whose husbands have been unfaithful, and thousands of men whose wives have lied to them. Satan whispers, "You don't need to forgive. You have a right to get even. They deserve to be punished."

Listen to me. That is a lie of the devil. When you refuse to forgive others, your heavenly Father will not forgive you, and your life will be destroyed by bitterness and hatred. Jesus said, "For if you forgive men for their transgressions, your heavenly Father will also forgive you. But if you do not forgive men, then your Father will not forgive your transgressions" (Matt. 6:14-15). Forgive your husband. Forgive your wife. Forgive one another. You can start over. Don't believe Satan's lies of vengeance. Receive the truth of forgiveness from Jesus instead.

Satan also attacks our minds by driving us to misuse our bodies through alcohol or other drugs. These substances deteriorate a person's capacity to resist evil. While on drugs, people can't think clearly. Their consciences are silenced. They commit sexual sins, robberies, even murders — things they would never think of doing in their right minds. But the craving for a substance controls their thoughts and actions, and the door is opened to demonic forces that are crouching in the wings — just waiting to pounce and destroy.

Take Every Thought Captive

So how do we win this battle for the mind? Paul wrote, "We are destroying speculations and every lofty thing raised up against the knowledge of God, and we are taking every thought captive to the obedience of Christ" (2 Cor. 10:5). Anytime you recognize a thought contrary to the Word of God, resist that thought and receive the truth.

Victory begins by knowing the Scriptures and Christ. When you know Jesus, you can take your thoughts to Him, and He will point out those that didn't come from Him. You will learn to recognize thoughts that don't match Christ's nature or the way He operates.

The Holy Spirit also enables you to discern the teachings you hear — whether they are truth or error, life or death. Don't focus on a teacher's method or delivery. Instead, ask the Holy Spirit, "Are the life and truth of God flowing through him?" This is the only way to discern between teachers who are sharing God's message and those sowing death in the lives of the hearers.

If we don't take our thoughts captive, the enemy will do so — and then we become his captives.

Submit to God

The Bible says: "But He [God] gives a greater grace. Therefore it says, 'God is opposed to the proud, but gives grace to the humble.' Submit therefore to God. Resist the devil and he will flee from you" (James 4:6-7).

There is a condition to our release from bondage: We first have to submit to God. We have to agree with God. We must admit we've sinned and given ground to the devil.

He's built a stronghold and is growing corrupt fruit in our lives. God says, Admit it. Humble yourself. Submit to God and then "resist the devil and he will flee from you. Draw near to God and He will draw near to you. Cleanse your hands, you sinners; and purify your hearts, you double-minded" (James 4:7b-8). We can't keep our focus on both God and religion, God and the world, God and pleasure, God and self. We've got to look to Jesus alone in repentance. That is submitting to God.

God used a carpet cleaner named Milton Green to bring deliverance to my life. I humbled myself, not caring that Milton saw me doing so. The important thing wasn't who saw me humbling myself, but before whom I was humbling myself. When, as a well-known evangelist living in defeat, I sat down in a chair at the request of a carpet cleaner, I humbled myself before almighty God. I humbled myself before the carpenter of Nazareth.

Until you humble yourself — admit you need help — you will not be delivered. Remember, God resists the proud and the arrogant.

Consider the woman who was bent double by a spirit in Luke 13. Remember how this woman was freed from a spirit of sickness? You'd think everyone who witnessed her deliverance would have been happy for her. Not so. Look at Luke 13:14: "And the synagogue official, indignant because Jesus had healed on the Sabbath, began saying to the multitude in response, 'There are six days in which work should be done; therefore come during them and get healed, and not on the Sabbath day.' "

That man refused to humble himself before God's act of healing. A woman who had been in bondage for eighteen years was set free! And instead of being happy for her the official was angry. That's pitiful — but that's the way a lot of people are. They don't want anything to happen unless it happens the way they think it should, when they think it should and to whom they think it should. They let people live in bondage, while they walk around in arrogance and defeat. They refuse to be humbled by the reality of spiritual warfare.

Listen to Jesus' response to the legalistic synagogue official: "You hypocrites, does not each of you on the Sabbath untie his ox or his donkey from the stall, and lead him away to water him? And this woman, a daughter of Abraham as she is, whom Satan has bound for eighteen long years, should she not have been released from this bond on the Sabbath day?" (Luke 13:15-16).

God comes to us in mercy and grace. He says, "I want to give you victory." We are to live as overcomers in this life. But we can only live as overcomers when we submit ourselves to Him.

How do we submit ourselves to God? By knowing the truth. Jesus said: "If you abide in My word, then you are truly disciples of Mine; and you shall know the truth, and the truth shall make you free" (John 8:31b-32). But knowing the truth is more than merely knowing truths. At some point, knowing truths leads us to ask whose definition of truth, whose teachings, we are going to accept. We will know many truths in our lives. But the essence of those truths is the truth which is Jesus. No one wins victory over the devil by accumulating sound doctrine. Victory comes through knowing Jesus and His Word.

The Pharisees had scriptural truths, but they weren't free. The same is true of people in church circles today. They dot every "i" and boast that they have all the truth. But they

91

are living a lie because their lives lack freedom or love. They don't even like people. When you receive God's truth, you're receiving Jesus and all the truths He proclaims — truths like loving God with all your heart, soul, mind and strength and truths like loving others as you love yourself.

David knew about both bondage and freedom. He committed some terrible deeds in his life, but he knew how to repent. He knew how to humble himself before God. That is why the Bible calls him "the man after God's own heart." He also understood the nature of the truth that transforms. He wrote about it in his great psalm of confession, Psalm 51:

> Behold, Thou dost desire truth in the innermost being, and in the hidden part Thou wilt make me know wisdom (v. 6).

God wants us to get the truth deep inside us. He wants it to change our characters from the inside out, to make us look like Jesus. This only happens when we receive Jesus and the things He stands for — Christ is the truth that will set us free.

Know Christ

I was in the middle of a lake trying to catch a fish one day, and I said, "God, how do you bind Satan? I've watched some people try to rebuke the devil, and often it didn't seem like anything happened."

Clearly and distinctly God answered, "You must have the mind of Christ."

As believers, we don't receive the spirit of the world; we

receive the Spirit of God. We discern the things of the Spirit which the natural man cannot discern (1 Cor. 2). Many times in Paul's writings he talks about having the mind of Christ. In his letter to the Romans he said, "Be transformed by the renewing of your mind, that you may prove what the will of God is, that which is good and acceptable and perfect" (12:2b). In Philippians Paul tells us to think about things that are true and pure (4:8). "Let this mind be in you, which was also in Christ Jesus," he says in Philippians 2:5 (KJV).

How do you bind Satan and stop evil thoughts? By having the mind of Christ.

To get the mind of Christ you must be born of the Spirit and become a new creation. You've got to receive Jesus. When with a childlike faith you receive Jesus into your heart as the One who died for your sins, you will have a new mind. Unfortunately, that mind may not always work in harmony with the mind of Christ. You must learn to submit your mind to Him, to humble yourself and depend on Him. As we discussed before, you've got to learn to recognize the thoughts that originate with Satan and resist them.

I've experienced this in my own life. My mother was raped, and from that union she conceived me. Even as a child my thoughts were impure and immoral. When Jesus redeemed me, I received a new mind, but those old patterns still came back to attack me on occasion. I had to have a continual renewing of my mind. How did I do that? Through Scripture.

Of course, Satan wars against God's Word. Jesus talks about this war in the parable of the sower of seeds (Matt. 13:1-23). The Word is sown, and Satan attacks it. Every time you hear the truth, the Word, Satan tries to snatch it away — or take you away from the truth. He'd rather have you arguing about Scripture than receiving life from it.

But you don't have to listen to the devil. Choose instead to listen to the Word and receive the truth. All it takes is time alone with God. Get to know Him. Fellowship with Him. Don't just spend time watching Christian television, listening to Christian tapes or reading Christian books, although these practices help. Nothing reprograms your mind with truth like spending time alone with God in His Word.

When you do this, you soon will learn to recognize anything that doesn't look or sound like Jesus and the Scriptures. Don't compare things with what your denomination teaches. Hold them to the light of Jesus and His Word. When something doesn't look and sound like Jesus, resist it and take it captive. Say in your mind and heart, "That was not of God. It was of the enemy. Lord, I resist it. I obey You. I have Your mind and Your truth." That's how you quench the fiery darts of the evil one and walk in victory, abiding in the Word of God. That is precisely what God wants for every one of His children. You can win the battle for the mind.

Paul described the choice we face: "For those who are according to the flesh set their minds on the things of the flesh, but those who are according to the Spirit, the things of the Spirit. For the mind set on the flesh is death, but the mind set on the Spirit is life and peace, because the mind set on the flesh is hostile toward God; for it does not subject itself to the law of God, for it is not even able to do so; and those who are in the flesh cannot please God" (Rom. 8:5-8).

We make choices. We choose life or death. We choose

truth or error. We choose God or Satan. We are constantly making these choices. And if we want our minds to be set on the Spirit, we need to take every thought captive, to submit to God, to learn His truth and to know Christ.

And, as we'll see in the next chapter, we need to put on the armor of God.

Summary

To win the battle for the mind we must realize that the objective is to bring every thought "captive to the obedience of Christ." The first requirement is a thorough knowledge of the Word of God. It is not enough to know the letter of the Word, however. We must submit to the Author, God Himself, and let Him guard our minds and protect our paths. Finally, we must know Christ and nurture an intimate, personal relationship with Him.

EIGHT

OUR ARMOR FROM GOD

SPIRITUAL WARFARE IS A VERY
constant reality. And though the war is difficult at times,
we can face the enemy without fear, confident that God
doesn't send us into battle unprotected. First of all, He
Himself is our fortress. God impressed this on me during
a recent church service. I was singing "A Mighty Fortress

Is Our God" with the congregation when the Lord said to me, "Listen to those words. I say I am a fortress. I am a stronghold, a shield. Did you ever stop to think what that implies? That says there's a war going on, and I and My presence are the only protection you have in this war."

In Psalm 18:1-2 we read: " 'I love Thee, O Lord, my strength.' The Lord is my rock and my fortress and my deliverer." He's not only our protection; He's our deliverer. He can deliver us from the hand of the enemy and secure us in the fortress. "My God, my rock, in whom I take refuge." Refuge from what? Refuge from the storm, from the problems, from the assault of the enemy. He's our protection.

God is also our hedge.

Remember when the devil came against Job? Satan said to God, "Hast Thou not made a hedge about him [Job] and his house and all that he has, on every side?" (Job 1:10a). Satan couldn't touch Job because of that hedge, which is God's glory, God's presence. When you abide in the Word, you have God's presence as a canopy over you and the shelter of the Almighty as a shield.

In addition to being our fortress and our hedge, God provides armor for us to wear in the battle. Much has been said and written about the Christian's armor described by Paul in Ephesians 6:11-18. But to make effective use of your weapons, it helps to know the purpose of each piece and how it functions to fulfill that purpose in the heat of battle.

First, be aware that your armor is "of God," or "from God." The armor and weapons you carry into battle were created by God, the most reliable supplier of armaments in the universe!

In the United States Army, the weapons and equipment

supplied each soldier are called "Government Issue," meaning they are the standard gear issued by the U.S. Government to its troops. From this came the term G.I., which became a nickname for the soldiers receiving the items. As a spiritual soldier, your gear is also G.I. — God Issue. It is the standard gear provided by God for all His troops. The same equipment was issued to Moses, Samson, Gideon, David and all the others to whom God gave great victory. It is the same gear used by Jesus Christ, the Lord and captain of our host!

American soldiers do not pay for their armor. To receive their G.I. weapons, all they have to do is identify themselves by name, rank and serial number. They simply have to know who they are. That's also the only requirement for obtaining spiritual armor. You just need to know you are a child of God, that your name is written in heaven because of your faith in Christ.

Because our weapons have been fashioned and issued by God, they are spiritual weapons. That means they are supernatural, capable of withstanding and overcoming the "principalities...powers...rulers of the darkness...spiritual wickedness in high places" (Eph. 6:12, KJV).

The first instruction we are given about our armor is to put it on. Without the armaments issued by the Lord, we have no chance against the enemy's supernatural schemes and devices. And we are told to put on "the whole armor," every piece of it. If you charge into battle without wearing every item of this armor, you will be vulnerable to Satan's deadly darts in some vital area. To put on your armor simply means to believe what God says about each piece and to use it faithfully for its intended purpose.

Now let's consider the various pieces of equipment and

the significance of each to spiritual victory.

Girdle of Truth or Reality

> Stand firm therefore, having girded your loins with truth... (Eph. 6:14).

The first piece of armor identified by Paul is the girdle. This is the broad strip of plating or mail the warrior buckles around his waist. It covers his hips, stomach and abdomen. It also serves as the anchor for other pieces of armor or for weapons, such as the sword and dagger, which are attached to it.

In spiritual warfare our girdle is truth. We know, of course, that God's Word is truth. But the Word of God is identified later as another part of the armament, the sword of the Spirit. The girdle of truth is best understood as the girdle of reality. Of course, we discover reality in the Scriptures. We must know the Word.

One of the keys to victory in any battle is the ability to keep a firm grip on reality. A soldier must maintain an awareness of the true situation and know what is going on. Many times in Old Testament battles God's enemies destroyed themselves because they lost touch with reality and became disoriented. In the confusion, they attacked each other.

By distorting truth, Satan has many Christians fighting one another. They have lost touch with the reality of who they are, who their friends are and who the real enemy is. One of the greatest dangers in spiritual warfare is attacking other believers rather than pursuing the enemy.

When you allow the Holy Spirit to teach you about truth

and reality, you can avoid this horrible deception. By holding firm to God's version of reality, you will always know what's happening on the battlefield. This solid sense of reality holds your armor in place, keeps your weapons handy for use and fends off the confusion and panic that could be your undoing once you enter the thick of the fight.

Breastplate of Righteousness

And having put on the breastplate of righteousness... (Eph. 6:14).

The Roman soldier wore two metal plates that protected his upper torso in front and back. These plates clamped together beneath his arms. The breastplate covered the heart, lungs and other vital organs. No soldier of Paul's day would have gone into battle without his breastplate in place. To do so would have been not only foolish but fatal!

The Christian's breastplate is his righteousness, or rather *His* righteousness. Righteousness from God. This righteousness, which we appropriate through faith (Rom. 10:3,6), becomes our own righteousness. In Christ we have been made the righteousness of God (2 Cor. 5:21). Unless you have your breastplate of righteousness, issued to you by God through faith, you are not likely to go into battle against the enemy at all. If you do, you will encounter almost instant defeat. Why? Because Satan most often attacks Christians with the powerful weapons of accusation and condemnation. When you plunge into battle, the enemy's first counterattack will usually be a fusillade of questions designed to undermine your confidence in your qualifications as a soldier of Christ. "What makes you think you're good

101

enough to war against me? You're not perfect, are you? Don't you feel just a little phony, claiming to be righteous? Didn't I see you sinning just a little while ago?"

You cannot withstand such an onslaught without your breastplate of righteousness — that is, until you believe that when God gave you new birth and made you a new creation, He also made you righteous. You are His workmanship (Eph. 2:10), and God's workshop doesn't produce unrighteousness.

Many churches emphasize sin too much and say too little about the righteousness Christ has given us. Because of this, many Christians have an unhealthy awareness of sin. What we need for effective spiritual warfare is just the opposite: a healthy awareness of our righteousness. This error in emphasis keeps Christians either cowering in fear behind the lines of battle or fleeing in panic after the first fiery dart whizzes toward them. If you don't know that your righteousness is secure, you won't have the courage for spiritual combat. You will spend your life hanging around the armory trying to create a breastplate that will stand the test of battle. You'll never succeed. The only righteousness that will sustain you is the righteousness "of God through faith." You cannot create that righteousness for yourself. It only comes through Jesus.

Once you have received your righteousness from Jesus, you have a breastplate that will deflect anything the enemy hurls at you. You can be confident of God's protection as you face the enemy in battle. Christ's righteousness will guard your heart.

Footwear — the Gospel of Peace

And having shod your feet with the preparation
of the gospel of peace... (Eph. 6:15).

It may seem strange that Paul mentions protection for the
feet in almost the same breath as armor for the heart and
lungs. But, being well aware of military operations and what
causes them to succeed or fail, Paul knew that an army goes
nowhere until its soldiers' feet are protected.

The Christian's footwear is the gospel of peace. The good
news that liberates captives from the enemy is what carries
you into battle. It's what saved you. It's what motivates you
to want others to be saved. It's what keeps you moving
forward against the enemy and his fortifications even when
the terrain is rough.

Today's Christian army often moves slowly and incon-
sistently because it isn't wearing the right shoes. The gospel
of peace is good news, but it is seldom presented as such.
Too often it comes across as bad tidings — toilsome works,
guilty burdens and unending tongue-lashings. With such
shoddy gear on his feet, no soldier is likely to venture
toward the battlefront. If he does, it won't be long before
he starts limping back to camp.

Putting the gospel of peace on your feet means receiving
by faith the good news of the New Testament. It is a
covenant based on grace, mercy and eternal life, not works,
condemnation and death. Now that's the kind of footwear
you can march on! Wearing the proper shoes, you can stomp
on the enemy. You can enter the battlefield knowing the evil
spirit world is under your control because of the authority
God has given you. That's peace.

The thought of being shod with the gospel of peace is all the more exciting when you realize that peace exists only after a battle has been fought and the enemy has been vanquished. Wearing the gospel of peace on our feet means having one foot planted on the back of our defeated foe while standing steadfast on the Word of God, through which we have been given the victory! The battle is already won! What greater confidence can there be than that?

The Shield of Faith

> Above all, taking the shield of faith... (Eph. 6:16, KJV).

That might better be read "over all" or "covering all." When the Roman soldier crouched behind his shield, it protected his entire body from head to foot. A group of Roman soldiers with their shields in place formed a protective wall against an enemy's spears, arrows and stones.

In the same way, faith covers everything for the Christian in combat. Faith actually provides the armor and the weapons and then protects each item — the girdle of truth, the breastplate of righteousness, the footwear of the gospel, the helmet of salvation, the sword of the Spirit. All depend on the shield of faith.

What is the shield of faith? Simply our belief in God, in His Word and in His promises. By believing what God has said, we know who we are, why we are engaged in this spiritual warfare, what we have to fight with and the ultimate triumphant outcome of the struggle.

As Paul says, the shield of faith quenches all the fiery darts of the wicked one. What are those fiery darts? They are Satan's lies, deceits and misrepresentations of reality. They are Satan's suggestions and accusations. When we use our shield of faith, we are believing God and rejecting the falsehoods flung at us by the enemy. All his fiery darts sputter and go out when we lift the truth of God against them. They lose their sting. They cannot penetrate our armor and inflict any wound upon us.

"Taking the shield of faith," Paul exhorts. That is a command to action. Faith is an action word. It is an exercise of the will, a deliberate act of choosing to believe God in the face of any conflicting statements or evidence.

You may consider yourself a believer, but before you go into battle be sure to check your shield. Do you really believe what God has said about who you are in Christ and the resources He has provided for waging spiritual war? If not, beware. Some of Satan's fiery darts of deceit may find the chinks in your armor.

We don't silence or kill the devil. However, we do destroy his effectiveness. His weapons look dangerous, but they are useless. Satan has only empty words and carefully polished lies that come like a barrage of flaming arrows against the church, the covenant people of God. All we need to do is recognize their origin, then take the shield of faith and extinguish them. Hold up the words of God as a shield to quench the lies and suggestions of Satan. Remember, those suggestions become fiery only when they lodge in our minds and hearts.

Helmet of Salvation

And take the helmet of salvation... (Eph. 6:17).

105

To win in battle, a soldier must not lose his head! Literally, of course, but spiritually as well. The helmet enables us to keep our heads, no matter how threatening and confusing the battle may be. It is our salvation. Putting on your helmet means knowing through faith and the confirmation of the Holy Spirit that you are saved. You know and believe the simple truth that salvation is from the Lord. It is the gift of God, by grace through faith, and not of works. You did nothing to earn it. You can do nothing to keep it. All you did was receive it, and that you did through a faith provided by God. God, and He alone, is able to keep it for you (2 Tim. 1:12).

If you don't put on your helmet of salvation, you will be confused in the thick of battle. You may doubt your salvation. You will be preoccupied with trying to do something to keep yourself saved. This self-centered activity will prevent you from waging an effective fight to destroy the enemy's works in your life and in the lives of others. Without a helmet, your mind will be exposed to every missile the enemy aims at you.

You must hear and believe what God says about your salvation. In doing so, you'll be putting on the helmet of salvation.

The Sword of the Spirit

And [take] the sword of the Spirit, which is the word of God (Eph. 6:17).

The sword of the Spirit is the last item on Paul's list of armaments, but it is by no means the least important. All the other pieces are strictly defensive. They protect you

106

from the enemy's weapons. The sword, the Word of God, is both offensive and defensive. You can use it to parry Satan's thrusts, as Jesus did during His wilderness temptation battle (Matt. 4:1-11), and you can also use it to put the enemy to flight and to set his captives free.

To use the sword effectively, however, you must avoid some common misconceptions. Using the sword does not mean merely reciting Scripture. The devil himself can, and does, quote Scripture.

Speaking to some Christians who were evidently quite adept at reciting Scripture and otherwise flaunting their "spirituality," Paul said, "But I will come to you soon, if the Lord wills, and I shall find out, not the words of those who are arrogant, but their power. For the kingdom of God does not consist in words, but in power" (1 Cor. 4:19-20; see also 1 Thess. 1:5).

Scripture clearly shows us that power is supplied by the Holy Spirit. The Word is, after all, the sword of the Spirit; only when wielded in union with the Spirit — through complete dependence on Him — can the Word go out in power. The apostles were instructed to wait in Jerusalem until they received the Holy Spirit. Only then would they have the power to perform their mission.

The key to using the Word effectively is, again, faith. The Word spoken in faith moves mountains (Mark 11:23). Using the Word in faith, Jesus stilled the wind and calmed the waves on the Sea of Galilee. In contrast, the disciples, reasoning without faith, concluded they were perishing in the same storm (Mark 4:35-41).

What happens when we use the Word without faith? This is best seen in the failure of the Israelites to go into the promised land. They had the Word, Hebrews 4:1 tells us, but it was of no use to them because they didn't combine it with faith. Because of their unbelief, their weapons were ineffective, and they failed to enter into God's rest — the wonderful peace that follows spiritual victory.

When wielded in faith, the sword may not be an exact quotation from Scripture, but it will be a word based on the promises of God as revealed in Scripture. On the lips of the spiritual warrior, any words so based and spoken in faith will activate the sword of the Spirit. And the enemy will not be able to withstand its power.

No better words sum up your capacity for spiritual warfare than those of the apostle Paul in 1 Corinthians 3:21 (NIV): "All things are yours." All things. Your identity as a child of God and a sharer of the heavenly calling, authority, power, weaponry and armor are all yours through Christ. You are fully equipped for spiritual battle. You can emerge victorious.

You Are a Conqueror

In light of all this, Paul's words in Romans 8:37 have a deeper significance. You are a conqueror! Nothing the enemy can throw at you can overcome you. No strength he can bring to bear is capable of resisting your power in Christ to destroy his works and free his captives.

There is one important thing to remember: All of this is true regardless of how you feel about it.

When the Lord appeared to Gideon (Judg. 6:12), He addressed him as a valiant warrior. Gideon didn't feel like a valiant warrior. He argued with the Lord, saying (my paraphrase): "My family is the poorest in all Israel, and I'm the poorest in the family. With such puny resources, how can I be mighty? And I'm not very brave either, Lord. Look where you've found me — hiding from the Midianites inside this winepress!''

But the Lord said, "I am with you." And He worked with Gideon, building his confidence until Gideon believed what God had said about him. Then he was able to prove himself a valiant warrior and to deliver the Israelites from their Midianite oppressors. How did he do it? By leading a mere 300 men, armed only with lamps, sticks and pitchers, against the Midianite horde numbering some 165,000. Because Gideon believed the Lord was with him, he defeated that great host in one battle and without drawing a sword! (See Judg. 6-8.)

You are valiant no matter how small and insignificant you may feel. "For we walk by faith, not by sight," Paul said (2 Cor. 5:7). That means we live according to what God says about things, not what we think or feel about them. That's faith, and faith "is the victory that has overcome the world" (1 John 5:4).

Let God introduce you to yourself. He says you are a valiant conqueror. Choose to believe Him. Live according to that belief, and you will experience the incomparable excitement and gratification that come with victory in spiritual warfare.

That doesn't mean you won't have some defeats. That doesn't mean you may not lose some battles, but you will be living in freedom as an overcomer. You will be rightly understanding the Word of truth and applying those teachings to your life so that the life of Christ is expressed in you.

If you feel inadequate, thank God for even that. He has to let us feel hopeless in our own ability before we will look to Him, hear His promise of "I am with you" and rely on His power to make us conquerors.

The Real Battlefield: Prayer and Petition

After exhorting us to put on the whole armor of God, Paul told us how to put it on, how to keep it on and how to use it most effectively in our warfare against the enemy and in defense of one another:

> With all prayer and petition pray at all times in the Spirit, and with this in view, be on the alert with all perseverance and petition for all the saints (Eph. 6:18).

Beware of making prayer a struggle. Knowing the necessity of prayer, many Christians have fallen into Satan's subtle trap of relying on the length, volume and eloquence of their prayers for victory in spiritual warfare. That kind of praying produces mental and physical fatigue. Jesus' invitation to rest applies to prayer as much as to any other area of our spiritual warfare.

It is the prayer of faith that releases the power of God. In prayer, as in anything else, faith is not works! To avoid the pitfall of the prayer struggle, it helps to recall that Jesus showed no strain when He performed some of His greatest miracles through prayer. Look at the feeding of the five thousand, the raising of Lazarus from the dead and the countless healings recorded in the Gospels.

Paul's very words in Ephesians 6 suggest a prayer of faith and rest, not one of works and struggle. No one could pray the laborious prayers that tax your mental and physical resources "all the time." Praying in the Spirit means yielding to His power and trusting in His wisdom. It means conversing with God on a spiritual level, not just begging Him for things that would serve selfish desires and purposes.

The prayer of faith is constant communion with God. It means trusting that God has welcomed you into His presence through Christ. It is constant awareness of your identity as a child of God. It means possessing an unwavering confidence that God knows your heart at all times and considers your every thought a prayer. It is an uninterrupted conversation with your Father — the loving heavenly Father who has assumed responsibility for your care (1 Pet. 5:7).

Live in an atmosphere of prayer and petition, praying at all times in the Spirit. That doesn't mean just praying in tongues. You can pray in tongues and not be praying in the Spirit; you can pray in English and pray in the Spirit. Jesus taught His disciples to pray the model prayer in a language they could understand. He never taught people to pray out of the Spirit. You don't always have to be praying in another language to be communicating with God. To pray in the Spirit means abiding in Christ, living in the Spirit. This is how to live in constant communication with God. We walk with God, talk with God, agree with God. We can discern our own thoughts, the influence of the spirits around us and the messages of the preachers and prophets who speak to us. We can discern the truth of God and avoid the lies of the devil.

111

You Are Not Alone

Paul's final instruction in Ephesians 6:18, "With this in view, be on the alert with all perseverance and petition for all the saints," contains an important reminder: none of us is alone in this spiritual combat. You are one warrior in a vast army of believers, and you have responsibilities for your comrades in arms.

You can look on things from the heavenly viewpoint. You are not "under the circumstances." You are "above," where your life is hidden with Christ in God (Col. 3:3). Knowing you are secure in Him, you are free to turn your attention to the needs of others. Be alert to those needs as a faithful soldier in combat, watching out for your buddies, warning them when they are in danger from the enemy, calling for supplies when they run low on ammunition or food, providing covering fire for them in the midst of battle, comforting them and giving first aid when they are wounded. If the response to your petitions seems long in coming, keep calling "with all perseverance" until the supplies and reinforcements arrive. Angels of darkness may block the aid that is sent, as when the "prince of the kingdom of Persia" delayed the angelic messenger who was responding to Daniel's prayer (Dan. 10:12-13). This is war. You must engage diligently in every phase of it! And you must act by faith.

Your battlefield responsibility doesn't stop with the warrior fighting at your side. It extends to the company, the battalion, the regiment, the division, the entire army of God. You are to "petition for all the saints."

Prayer and petition are the keys to success on the spiritual battlefield. And our standing with God, our confidence before the throne of grace, is the key to success in prayer and petition; for it is whatsoever we ask in prayer, believing, not begging or struggling for, that we receive. And the most important thing we receive is victory.

Summary

God has supplied us with every spiritual weapon we could possibly need to war against the powers of darkness. In describing these weapons, Paul used the armor of the Roman soldier of his day as the model. Our spiritual armor includes the girdle of truth about our midsection, the breastplate of righteousness, the gospel of peace as our footwear, the shield of faith, the helmet of salvation and the sword of the Spirit. We are commanded to put on all of this armor before entering the fray. Putting it on is a simple act of faith. We merely choose to believe that we have it, as God says we do. Having done that, we can go into battle — but not alone. As individuals, we're each part of an army, and God directs us to join hands with one another to oppose the enemy and to support one another in the battle.

N I N E

CALLED TO DELIVER

IT IS IRONIC THAT SOME CHRISTIANS regard deliverance and healing as controversial, things to be approached with caution, skepticism or even hostility. This is a work of the enemy to blind and confuse believers. By fueling doubts about deliverance and healing, he hinders our part of the battle. In reality the enemy steals, kills and destroys; he captivates and afflicts. Believers heal and deliver.

What is deliverance? It is confronting demons in the power of the Holy Spirit. It involves casting demons out of those who are demon-possessed, liberating believers from demonic oppression and harassment, and taking other actions designed to overcome the forces of darkness.

The Example of Jesus

Jesus' ministry demonstrated this activity and revealed it to be a vital and continuing function of the kingdom of God. In fact, deliverance was one of the first acts of Jesus after He began His ministry.

In Mark 1 Jesus enters a synagogue to preach. As He presents the gospel, an unclean spirit manifests itself in a member of the congregation. Jesus commands the demon to be quiet and come out of the man, and "throwing [the man] into convulsions, the unclean spirit cried out with a loud voice, and came out of him" (Mark 1:26). Jesus said He gave us that same authority (Matt. 10:1; Luke 10:17). The only way to learn about deliverance is from Jesus Christ. Jesus teaches you how to live the truth, performing the ministry of God.

How did the people respond to Jesus' act of deliverance? "And they were all amazed, so that they debated among themselves" (Mark 1:27). Onlookers questioned the phenomenon then just as they do today. But exercising power over Satan and his forces was clearly a strategic part of Jesus' earthly ministry. In Mark 1:34 it is listed along with physical healing as a standard element of His ministry.

Jesus described His ministry of deliverance to the people

in His hometown synagogue: " 'The Spirit of the Lord is upon Me, because He anointed Me to preach the gospel to the poor. He has sent Me to proclaim release to the captives, and recovery of sight to the blind, to set free those who are downtrodden, to proclaim the favorable year of the Lord' " (Luke 4:18-19). He came first to preach the gospel, but what is the gospel? The good news, God's plan of salvation. And what does it mean to be saved? To be redeemed, set free, delivered from the hand of the enemy.

The next phrases in the passage all refer to deliverance in some respect. To proclaim release to the captives is patently an act of deliverance. To give sight to the blind is deliverance from spiritual darkness and ignorance, as well as from physical sightlessness. To set free the oppressed or downtrodden is another obvious act of deliverance. And to proclaim the favorable year of the Lord, the Jubilee year, is an act of delivering the person as well as anything else Satan has plundered.

How did the hometown people respond to Jesus' message in Luke 4? They remembered Him as Joseph's boy and would not accept Him as a prophet. When Jesus confronted their attitude and reminded them that God sometimes sent His prophets to help gentiles rather than Jews, they got mad and tried to kill Him.

If you walk in the Spirit, expect to experience some of these things. You will be mistreated — Jesus was. But don't react in anger if the religious crowd rejects you when you walk in truth. Don't get puffed up and critical; don't pull out with your little group. Keep loving those who are unkind, reaching out to them. They are being defeated, so don't join their ranks by acting as they do.

Jesus escaped the people in Nazareth and went to Capernaum, where He again taught in the synagogue (Luke 4:30-31). He met a man possessed by an evil spirit. What did Jesus do? He rebuked the demon, and it left the man. Jesus again showed His authority over the enemy. But Jesus didn't always rebuke demons. Look what happened next. "And He arose and left the synagogue, and entered Simon's home. And Simon's mother-in-law was suffering from a high fever; and they made request of Him on her behalf. And standing over her, He rebuked the fever, and it left her" (Luke 4:38-39).

Sometimes Jesus rebuked spirits; sometimes He rebuked sickness. He didn't always do it the same way, so we shouldn't either. Don't get trapped by some formula for deliverance; be led of the Spirit.

The Spirit who led Jesus to the wilderness to be tempted by the devil also gave Jesus the answers He needed to defeat the devil. The Spirit who enabled Jesus to walk in victory as the Son of the living God is the same Spirit who will lead you. Jesus didn't follow a formula. He did whatever the Father told Him to do because spiritual victory always grows out of a relationship with God and obedience to Him.

The ministry of Jesus is summed up in Hebrews 2:14-15 as a ministry of deliverance: "That through death He might render powerless him who had the power of death, that is, the devil; and might deliver those who through fear of death were subject to slavery all their lives."

Called to Deliver

Hebrews 3:1 goes on to reveal that all of Christ's holy brothers and sisters — all true believers — are partakers of that heavenly calling. We call Christ the deliverer, and rightly so. But in Christ we are all deliverers and are called to deliver!

When I first started learning to talk to the devil, my pride said, I hope nobody hears you doing that. Funny thing was, there wasn't anyone who was going to hear but the devil — he's the one who didn't want "anyone" to hear. He didn't want his legions to hear me because in Jesus' name I've got authority over them. That's what Jesus said. We can talk to the evil forces and tell them to go.

How do you rebuke evil spirits? You say, "Be quiet and come out." It's not volume, but it is authority. You can say to evil spirits, "You can't have my kids. You will not have my kids." Don't fuss at your children. Tell those vile spirits of rebellion, selfishness and compulsion, "You'll not have my kid." Rebuke those spirits. You don't necessarily do this in the presence of your children. Sometimes it's best to do it alone in prayer. Other times you may say to your child, "I'm going to talk to those spirits." Let the Holy Spirit show you which is best.

Don't be afraid of demons. Jesus didn't give us a spirit of fear; He gave us love, power and a sound mind. If you receive a spirit of fear, you'll not be able to deliver other people. You'll need to be delivered first so you can go out and deliver others, in obedience to the Lord.

We also are called to heal the sick. The Bible says in Acts 10:38, "You know of Jesus of Nazareth, how God anointed Him with the Holy Spirit and with power, and how He went about doing good, and healing all who were oppressed by the devil; for God was with Him." As we discussed in an earlier chapter, this doesn't mean all sickness comes from demonic oppression — but some sickness does. Jesus commissioned us to follow His example and heal the sick.

Start speaking to sickness and tell it to go. Start speaking to disease. Whether you see an instant miracle or not, rejoice because God is still God. Love Him with all your heart and act on His Word. As you act in obedience to God's Word, supernatural results will follow. You will be casting out demons. You will be setting captives free. You will see healing power begin to flow.

Become a True Disciple

Many Christians are fond of quoting John 8:32: "You shall know the truth, and the truth shall make you free." But that verse can't be separated from the one preceding it, where Jesus told those who believed Him, "If you abide in My Word, then you are truly disciples of Mine."

Clearly, one of the foremost characteristics of a disciple is that he has been set free and follows Christ's command to make other disciples. To do this he must know how to set others free. That is deliverance in the broadest sense of the term.

The truth will make you free only if you believe it, if you take Jesus' word that the things He tells you are real and if you "abide" in it — act on the truth in your daily life.

God has shown us who we are in Christ. We are His children, Christ's brethren and joint-heirs with Him (Rom. 8:16-17). We are strengthened with might according to His glorious power (Col. 1:11). In Him we are always marching in God's victory parade (2 Cor. 2:14). We are more than conquerors (Rom. 8:37), because Christ Himself is our life (Col. 3:4): "When Christ, who is our life, is revealed, then you also will be revealed with Him in glory."

But how many Christians believe that and live accord-

120

ingly? God created us to be overcomers; He has given us the power to be overcomers. And the victory that overcomes the world is our faith (1 John 5:4). Believe what Jesus said and do it. You will bring the kingdom of God, with all its victory, joy, peace and freedom, into the realm of present reality.

Exert Authority Over the Enemy

Jesus said, "I will give you the keys of the kingdom of heaven; and whatever you shall bind on earth shall be bound in heaven, and whatever you shall loose on earth shall be loosed in heaven" (Matt. 16:19).

Much of the church is blind to the tremendous authority delegated to us in this verse, because it has been interpreted strictly as a reference to our ultimate salvation. Actually, that interpretation makes no sense. Is anything going to be bound in heaven, where all believers will live with Jesus after they leave their mortal bodies? If nothing is bound there, then what would be loosed there?

The reference is to the church — which Jesus has just told Peter and the other disciples that He will build — and its authority in this present world. The church, all disciples, will be given the keys of the kingdom of heaven. With those keys they will go out into the world locking up and imprisoning some things, and unlocking and setting free other things.

These actions will be taken "on earth," that is, in the visible realm, in mortal bodies — but the effects of those actions are carried out in the invisible realm where the spiritual forces exist and operate. "The keys of the kingdom" is simply the authority given believers in this world to get things done in the spiritual domain.

When a disciple exercises his authority by speaking with an audible voice, his commands are carried out in the invisible spiritual realm. If he orders a demon to be bound and removed from a place or a person, he may not see the demonic being or any visible evidence of the spiritual action taking place. But it will be done as he has commanded.

That's what happened in my deliverance. After Milton Green commanded the demons to be bound and ordered me to be loosed, he asked if I felt anything. I had not. There was no evidence "on earth," in the visible realm, that anything had happened. But two days later I realized I was no longer bound — I had been set free. Plenty had taken place in the invisible realm.

Pay close attention here: If you're a Christian, you've got that same authority. You can speak to the enemy who is tormenting someone, and the enemy will leave! First, pray with love for the person. Pray about who they are in Christ. Then acknowledge the defeat they are living in and their desire to be delivered. Speak to the spirits, calmly yet with authority rebuking those that the Holy Spirit reveals to you.

I have seen the keys of the kingdom used countless times, binding and loosing in the visible realm with consequences in the invisible realm. I've seen it happen in my wife's life.

After I was delivered, the enemy tried to come against me again through Betty. She became irritated and resentful toward me. She took it as an affront when I was away for long periods, although she knew I had to be gone to do the work God had called me to. She felt neglected when I did things without her, even when I spent time with the children.

One evening I went jogging with our daughter Rhonda.

When we got back home, Betty was fuming. I had never seen her react with such irrational fury.

During dinner one night, a Spirit-filled friend who was visiting us noticed Betty's countenance and said to me, "Can I show you that the most precious person you know needs deliverance in some areas of her life?" I was embarrassed. But I knew this man knew about spiritual authority, so I told him to go ahead.

After talking to Betty for a few minutes, he began to speak to the enemy with authority. The enemy manifested himself. God will allow demons to manifest themselves only when their captive is submitting to Him, so that God will be glorified by the manifestation. In this instance Betty's entire body began to shake. She trembled so violently the whole dinner table shook.

"Stop right now; that's enough!" our friend commanded. The shaking stopped, and he told Betty to relax.

Turning to me, he said, "A spirit of fear is clinging to something in your wife's life. There is something between you and your wife, and the spirit of fear is holding on to some deeper root problem, a stronghold the enemy has been able to build in her mind."

Later Betty and I got alone in prayer, and the Spirit revealed that the stronghold of fear was built in her childhood. She had been frightened by many things as she grew up. She used to lie in terror at night, thinking the bedpost was going to come down and kill her.

Now the same spirit of fear was convincing her she would lose me. The enemy had convinced her that she was not worthy to be my wife. He had told her I could have done much better in choosing a wife, that she wasn't good enough or pretty enough to be my wife. He had said she would die and be removed from the picture so I could get a more suitable mate.

Once we identified the problem, Betty and I spoke with authority against the oppressing demonic spirits and commanded the strongholds to be destroyed. In the invisible realm those orders were carried out, and that was one of the most glorious days any two people ever spent together.

Renew Your Mind

Deliverance from spirits is wonderful, but the battle doesn't end there. Those who have been delivered must continue to oppose the enemy's influence in their lives by renewing their minds. Jesus issued a strong warning about this struggle in Matthew 12:

> "Now when the unclean spirit goes out of a man, it passes through waterless places, seeking rest, and does not find it. Then it says, 'I will return to my house from which I came'; and when it comes, it finds it unoccupied, swept, and put in order. Then it goes, and takes along with it seven other spirits more wicked than itself, and they go in and live there; and the last state of that man becomes worse than the first" (vv. 43-45).

When you've prayed for someone, the evil spirit has gone, and deliverance and salvation have occurred. However, if the person's "house" is not occupied, he becomes even more vulnerable to the enemy's attack. God's presence and the Holy Spirit must fill his life, which will bring him the impenetrable shield of God's glory.

What happens when someone's "house" remains unoccupied? The evil spirit who was driven out goes and gets seven other spirits more evil than he is. Together they attack and oppress the man who was delivered, and, as Jesus said, "the last state of that man becomes worse than the first."

When you humble yourself, when you submit to God, when you resist the devil, do it with earnestness and diligence. Look to Jesus. Keep receiving Him. He is the deliverer, and He's the One who can keep you walking in freedom.

Before I met Milton Green, God had used two other godly men to lead me through deliverance. They gave me some Scripture verses and said, "You need to read these and renew your mind, because if you don't renew your mind, you won't make it."

Back at the hotel room where Betty and I were staying, I said, "Something wonderful happened to me today. I believe I'm walking in a freedom I haven't known since the first days of my ministry. It's wonderful."

I went back home and told my friends what had happened to me. I told them I had been under demonic assault. Some of them mocked me, humiliated me and put me down for believing in such "nonsense." They hurt me so badly I didn't even read the written material and Bible verses I'd been given.

Because I did not walk on with Jesus, the evil spirits that released me came back and brought seven more with them. I'm not exaggerating when I tell you I stepped from a fire into an absolute inferno. During the next few years I was so miserable I prayed to die. You see, I had turned my back on the deliverance God had given me. I did not walk on with Him into a life of victory over the enemy.

125

It would be better for you not to hear the truth than to hear it, respond to it and turn your back on it. That's why once a person has been delivered he not only needs a refreshing from God's presence, but a continual renewal. He needs to pursue the transformation of the mind that Paul mentions in Romans 12:1-2 (Phillips): "With eyes wide open to the mercies of God, I beg you, my brothers, as an act of intelligent worship, to give him your bodies, as a living sacrifice, consecrated to him and acceptable by him. Don't let the world around you squeeze you into its own mould, but let God re-mould your minds from within, so that you may prove in practice that the plan of God for you is good, meets all his demands and moves towards the goal of true maturity."

Pursue the Enemy

Once you are delivered, don't stop until you grind the enemy into dust. Pursue him. This simply means to get honest. If you are released from certain sins but know you are still vulnerable in those areas, call together some spiritual warriors who understand the authority Jesus has given us. When those areas of weakness rise up again, agree together in prayer against them. Humble yourself and get all the help you need; every single one of us in the name of Jesus can turn every one of those enemies to dust. That's how to pursue the enemy.

Have you been delivered? Don't just say, I've got relief. Continue seeking release and strength so you can keep walking over the enemy! We don't need a spiritual bubble bath; we need a thorough scrubbing from the enemy's influence. Then we need to be sanctified in the Word.

Most of us live lives of restraint with regard to sin. We tough it out. We tell God we won't sin, and we keep a stiff upper lip. We think, I want to do it so badly, but I won't. I'm going to do what's right if it kills me. Is it any wonder we're so tired? Self-imposed restraint will always make you tired.

Jesus doesn't teach us restraint, and He didn't come to give us relief. He came to release the captives. Once we are free from the enemy's influence, we can flee to the refuge provided by Jesus. Then, in the power of the Holy Spirit, we can pursue the enemy until we flatten him under our feet.

Read what the psalmist said:

> I pursued my enemies and overtook them, and I did not turn back until they were consumed....I shattered them, so that they were not able to rise; they fell under my feet....Thou hast also made my enemies turn their backs to me, and I destroyed those who hated me. They cried for help, but there was none to save, even to the Lord, but He did not answer them. Then I beat them fine as the dust before the wind; I emptied them out as the mire of the streets (Ps. 18:37-42).

One more thing. Never betray the confidence of Christians who have asked you to help them pursue the enemy. If you are working with someone who needs more help than you alone can offer, get their permission before you include others in the battle.

A Picture of Restoration

Once we have been delivered, we can find restoration in those areas of our lives where Satan formerly held us in bondage. Consider the picture of restoration in Joel 2. In the first chapter of Joel the enemy attacks the people of God in the form of locusts stripping all the fruitfulness from the fields: "What the gnawing locust has left, the swarming locust has eaten; and what the swarming locust has left, the creeping locust has eaten; and what the creeping locust has left, the stripping locust has eaten" (Joel 1:4).

That's exactly what the powers of darkness have done to Christians today. The body of Christ has been stripped of fruitfulness. Christians show up at church regularly, but there's no fruit. That's the work of the devil. He strips away the beauty of Jesus, removing our joy and peace.

God says if you will repent, if you will turn to Him, He'll restore all the years, all the fruit, that the locusts ate up. When God delivered me, that was one of the first things that concerned me. I prayed, "God, I know I missed You, and I failed. I let the fear of man affect me; I became religious and selfish. Can You still use me? Lord, do I have a future? Or are You just going to use somebody else?"

Some of you are asking the same things. You think it's too late. Your chance for service is gone. There's no hope. Listen! God has a word for you, a wonderful word: " 'Yet even now,' declares the Lord, 'Return to Me with all your heart, and with fasting, weeping, and mourning; and rend your heart and not your garments' " (Joel 2:12).

Don't merely go through the motions of repentance. Rend your heart. Come with inner brokenness, with a contrite heart. Confess to God that you need help, that you missed

Him, that you didn't know. Or, if such is the case, confess that you willingly sinned, that you were selfish and you knew it. Whatever your story is, confess it to God. Get the truth of repentance inside; say it with your heart, and out of the abundance of your heart let your mouth speak.

When you have done this, the Lord has these words for you: "Now return to the Lord your God, for He is gracious and compassionate, slow to anger, abounding in lovingkindness, and relenting of evil" (Joel 2:13). Look especially at verse 18: "Then the Lord will be zealous for His land, and will have pity on His people. And the Lord will answer and say to His people, 'Behold, I am going to send you grain, new wine, and oil, and you will be satisfied in full with them; and I will never again make you a reproach among the nations. But I will remove the northern army far from you, and I will drive it into a parched and desolate land....' "

God says, "I'm going to drive the enemy out. I'm going to deliver you." Listen to this glorious promise in verses 23-25:

> So rejoice, O sons of Zion, and be glad in the Lord your God; for He has given you the early rain for your vindication....The early and the latter rain as before. And the threshing floors will be full of grain, and the vats will overflow with the new wine and oil. "Then I will make up to you for the years that the swarming locust has eaten, the creeping locust, the stripping locust, and the gnawing locust...."

God wants to return to you everything Satan and this

world have stolen. He wants to pour out on you the former and the latter rain at the same time. He wants to give you joy unspeakable. He wants to give you peace beyond understanding. He wants to give you total release in His Spirit. He wants to fill you with a supernatural love — He wants to make you look just like Jesus.

Summary

To be victorious, we must be delivered from all demonic captivity. The ministry of Jesus reveals deliverance to be one of the principal activities of the Christian's calling. Engaging in deliverance requires Christians to become true disciples, well-versed in the truth that sets people free. We must know our authority in Christ and be bold in exerting it over the enemy. When deliverance has been achieved, we must continue to resist the enemy by helping to renew the mind of the delivered one. We must pursue the enemy and trample him to a powder, assuring that he can never return and regain control. Then we can experience God's exciting work of restoration in all the areas once held by the enemy.

T E N

FOCUS ON CHRIST

IT'S NOT ENOUGH TO BE DELIVERED from the enemy. You must focus on Christ. As the writer of Hebrews urged, "Let us run with endurance the race that is set before us, fixing our eyes on Jesus, the author and perfecter of faith, who for the joy set before Him endured the cross, despising the shame, and has sat down at the right hand of the throne of God. For consider Him who has endured such hostility by sinners against Himself, so that you may not grow weary and lose heart" (12:1b-3).

Following Jesus means practicing His life-style. Every time the Holy Spirit blows the whistle and says, "You've missed the Word; you've missed the will of God," stop and repent. If you don't repent, you'll be vulnerable to the enemy.

Even football teams know the importance of following the rules. If a team persists in breaking the rules, it gets more and more penalties, thus giving up more and more ground and losing the game. So it is in the lives of believers who are not serious about their relationships with Jesus. They lose ground to the devil. Our only strength is in Jesus.

Regain Your First Love

When you receive Christ, you are a new creation. You live full of love and joy and peace. You are an overcomer. You love God with all your heart. That's the norm. That's what God wants for you. But most Christians live much of their lives defeated by the enemy. They know God, but something has happened. How many Christians do you know who really witness about Jesus, or who have such a zeal for God — such compassion for souls — that their testimonies can't be silenced?

Most Christians can't be stirred to speak about what they've heard. Most church people are terrified to witness. Too few are sold out for the Lord. What has gone wrong? They are like the church at Ephesus. Jesus sent a message to that church in the book of Revelation: "But I have this against you, that you have left your first love" (2:4).

Jesus went on to tell the church at Ephesus, "Remember therefore from where you have fallen, and repent and do the deeds you did at first; or else I am coming to you, and will remove your lampstand out of its place — unless you repent" (Rev. 2:5).

The lampstand represents the Ephesian church (Rev. 1:20). Jesus was saying that if the church did not repent and return to its first love, it would no longer overcome darkness with light. It would be defeated. When you love Christ with all your heart and soul and mind and strength, the evil spirit world knows who is in control. The kingdom of heaven is at hand. You can overcome the enemy. But if you lose that love, you will be overcome. We must regain our first love for Jesus.

Know the Truth

As we know Jesus, we also know truth. "I am the way, and the truth, and the life; no one comes to the Father, but through Me," Jesus said (John 14:6). Knowing truth — knowing Jesus — helps us recognize Satan's lies and respond to situations as Jesus would. We are overcomers.

Too often we try to overcome the enemy in our own strength. We rely on human understanding, programs and rules to protect us from sin. This gets our focus off Jesus and leaves us open to enemy attack. Paul warned us about this very clearly:

> Therefore let no one act as your judge in regard to...things which are a mere shadow of what is to come; but the substance belongs to Christ. Let no one keep defrauding you of your prize by delight-

> ing in self-abasement and the worship of the angels, taking his stand on visions he has seen, inflated without cause by his fleshly mind, and not holding fast to the head....If you have died with Christ to the elementary principles of the world, why...do you submit yourself to decrees, such as, "Do not handle, do not taste, do not touch!"...in accordance with the commandments...of men? These are matters which have...the appearance of wisdom in self-made religion and self-abasement and severe treatment of the body, but are of no value against fleshly indulgence (Col. 2:16-23).

When we think we know the answer to everything, we're in trouble. We're not open to the truth of God. We're not open to the fresh moving of the Spirit, the fresh revelation of Jesus. I'm not talking about additional revelation or adding to the Word; I'd never suggest that. I mean real illumination, real inspiration, real revelation of who Jesus is.

Great preachers and teachers in the church often live their lives in arrogance. Some of the most defeated people you could meet are people who think they've learned it all. They have theological systems that are air-tight. They have an answer for everything. They've got truths, but they don't have *the* truth, Jesus Christ.

When Jesus prayed for His disciples, He said, "I praise Thee, O Father, Lord of heaven and earth, that Thou didst hide these things from the wise and intelligent and didst reveal them to babes. Yes, Father, for thus it was well-pleasing in Thy sight" (Luke 10:21b). God doesn't reveal spiritual truth to the proud and arrogant. He reveals it to the humble. It wasn't some highly educated person who prayed for me to be delivered. It was an uneducated man. By following Jesus, Milton Green had discovered that Christians have authority over evil spirits, and he was willing to live out that truth.

Jesus said, "Therefore everyone who hears these words of Mine, and acts upon them, may be compared to a wise man, who built his house upon the rock. And the rain descended, and the floods came, and the winds blew, and burst against that house; and yet it did not fall, for it had been founded upon the rock" (Matt. 7:24-25).

Christ is the rock; building your house on the rock means hearing and obeying His words. You read about Jesus' ways, words and works, and you know truth. When you read the Bible as a love letter rather than a textbook, you will start to know Jesus. But the enemy is trying to block you from knowing Jesus. He will try to distract you, deceive you and destroy you. Don't let him.

Discern the Spirits

First John 2:26-27 says: "These things I have written to you concerning those who are trying to deceive you. And as for you, the anointing which you received from Him abides in you, and you have no need for anyone to teach you; but as His anointing teaches you about all things, and is true and is not a lie, and just as it has taught you, you abide in Him."

In Jesus we have the Holy Spirit's anointing to discern and defeat evil spirits, to disperse the enemy. The Holy Spirit teaches us. The antichrist spirit strives to get our eyes off Jesus and onto something else. But if we keep our eyes on Jesus, we will be able to discern spirits and live in victory.

In Luke 4 Jesus encountered Satan. The devil quoted Scripture, distorting its meaning in an effort to get Jesus to sin. Be aware that the enemy uses Scripture to manipulate you, while God uses Scripture to stimulate you to good works. There's a vast difference between those two uses of Scripture.

Throughout His temptation Jesus knew the truth, and that enabled Him to be free. There is a Scripture, a truth, for every situation. You cannot discern the spirits and the reality of the spiritual realm if you are a stranger to the Scriptures. You must study the Word. Further, you must reject anything — even something in your denomination — that does not line up with God's Word. When you do that, you will "walk in a manner worthy of the Lord, to please Him in all respects, bearing fruit in every good work and increasing in the knowledge of God" (Col. 1:10b). God wants you to be fruitful. He wants you to be full of love and joy and peace and goodness and kindness and faithfulness and temperance. He wants you to be winning others to Christ. This is the fruit in which you and I are to abound.

We're to be "strengthened with all power, according to His glorious might, for the attaining of all steadfastness and patience; joyously giving thanks to the Father, who has qualified us to share in the inheritance of the saints in light. For He delivered us from the domain of darkness, and transferred us to the kingdom of His beloved Son" (Col. 1:11-13).

This is the supernatural power of God: not people ruling on this earth, but God ruling in our lives. Knowing Christ and living out His truth is kingdom life. It's a present possibility, and it can be reality for you right now.

Unite With Other Believers

The closer we get to Jesus, the closer we will get to one another. We need that relationship with other members of the body. It is through them that Jesus ministers to us.

Never allow differences and disagreements with other believers to cause a break in fellowship. When you cut yourself off from other Christians, you're cutting yourself off from Jesus. Just because some parts of the body are not healthy doesn't mean you should cut them off. Minister to them.

If you differ with other Christians over Scripture and are convinced your position is right, don't condemn and accuse them. Don't set yourself up as their judge. If you do, you will be opposing God's eternal purposes and intentions. If you don't have love, you're nothing but a loud noise (1 Cor. 13:1). We must live in love. That is the most important part of God's will.

The Sufficiency of the Cross

And when you were dead in your transgressions and the uncircumcision of your flesh, He made you alive together with Him, having forgiven us all our transgressions, having canceled out the certificate of debt consisting of decrees against us and which was hostile to us; and He has taken it out of the way, having nailed it to the cross. When He had disarmed the rulers and authorities, He

137

made a public display of them, having triumphed
over them through Him (Col. 2:13-15).

Jesus disarmed the enemy through His work on the cross.
Let's look at the weapons that have been stripped from
Satan.

First, the law was fulfilled, so the devil can't accuse us
with it or use it against us. He wants to hold it over our
heads and say, "Since you've broken the law, you deserve
to be punished." He tries to control us by accusing and
condemning us. But when Jesus died on the cross, He
fulfilled the law and paid our penalty. If you know this
truth — and really believe it — Satan cannot use the law
against you.

Second, sin was defeated. All your sins — past, present
and future — were forgiven in Christ Jesus. The devil tries
to condemn you by reminding you of your sins, but he can't
use them against you if you know the truth.

Third, when Jesus died and rose again three days later,
death was defeated as well. The cross has disarmed the
devil.

If I stuck a gun in your chest and said, "Give me your
money, or I'll shoot you," you would probably give me your
money. But if you knew there were no bullets in my gun,
you'd say, "Get out of my way." That's the way we can treat
Satan. He is a bluffer. Unless you believe him, he is
powerless. He does not have the authority to do anything
to believers. That authority belongs to Jesus, and He has
given it to us.

Nothing Will Injure Us

Jesus said, "Behold, I have given you authority to tread upon serpents and scorpions, and over all the power of the enemy, and nothing shall injure you" (Luke 10:19).

Do you know what that means? If you're walking in obedience to the Lord and in submission to His Word, all things will work together for good. Pain, persecution, tragedy and crises may come, but if you keep your eyes on Jesus, God will use these things to form the character of Christ in you. He will transform your mind so that the difficult experiences make you more like Jesus. Remember: He never said you would not experience hurt or pain. He said nothing will be able to injure you — not if you view it with His eternal purposes in mind.

The devil will try to get you to say, "God's not fair. The whole world's falling apart. My life is caving in." Well, when Jesus was hanging on the cross, His whole life seemed to be caving in. It looked as if His whole ministry had been a disastrous failure. Satan thought he had the Son of God right where he wanted Him. Jesus had been captured and convicted of blasphemy in an illegal trial; His disciples had fled for their lives; the Romans mocked Christ, drove spikes through His wrists and thrust a spear into His side; the people of Jerusalem mocked Him and asked Him for one more miracle.

Yet, in spite of it all, God was still God. He never lost control then, and He never loses control now. Christ was victorious because He kept His focus on the eternal purposes of God. Satan experienced final defeat because he did not understand those purposes.

If you want to live in victory over the enemy, you've got

to see that God is always in control. No matter what comes your way, God will use it for good if you let Him. He will make you more like Jesus. Nothing will injure you. Jesus has given you authority over all the power of the enemy.

Rejoice in Who You Are in Christ

As important as our authority in Christ is, it's not the most important thing in our lives. Jesus said, "Nevertheless do not rejoice in this, that the spirits are subject to you, but rejoice that your names are recorded in heaven" (Luke 10:20).

I've seen people be delivered then fall back into absolute defeat and deception because they didn't keep their focus on Jesus. Don't rejoice in what you can do in Jesus' name. Rejoice in who you are in His name. Base your joy on your relationship with Him, not what that relationship may bring you.

Intimacy with Jesus is the only thing that will keep us living in victory. Martha was busy working for Jesus, but Mary was sitting at His feet listening to Him. Jesus said, "Martha, Martha, you are worried and bothered about so many things; but only a few things are necessary, really only one, for Mary has chosen the good part, which shall not be taken away from her" (Luke 10:41b-42).

You are a part of the family of God. Rejoice! And rejoice that you're in relationship with Christ, that you are living in His light and in the power of the Spirit. That's what gives us the victory — the only victory that really matters.

Summary

Focusing on Jesus is the ultimate key to victory. Our strength is in Him. Christians need to regain their first love for the Savior. The truth sets us free, but the truth is not a body of knowledge — it's Jesus Himself. God has given us an anointing that allows us to discern and defeat evil spirits. We can march on to victory by uniting with other believers and recognizing that Jesus, through the cross, has already disarmed the enemy and crushed his power. We can rejoice in the victory He has given us and in who we are in Christ.

CONCLUSION

THE HYPE PRECEDING MAJOR sporting events such as the Olympics, the World Series, the Final Four in college basketball and the Superbowl puts the competitors in a euphoric state of anticipation. That's understandable. To the victor goes the trophy and the ensuing glory.

We have all the more reason to be excited about conquering the enemy of almighty God in the power of His Spirit.

My close friend Dudley Hall shared an illustration that I think clearly depicts how we should regard spiritual warfare.

As a college student at Samford University in Alabama on a football scholarship, he practiced the sport each day of the week under careful coaching instruction.

All of the players routinely worked out and ran plays until they could move the ball with precision. Dudley said, "Our goal was to advance the leather football across a white chalk line, known as the goal line. We carefully worked at our offensive intentions and our defensive strategies. We were as dedicated and determined as any military strategists facing the expected fury of enemy armies.

"We ran drill after drill until our abilities were honed to perfection. We could really move the ball down the field and across the goal line with the greatest of ease."

Then, each weekend, a strange thing happened. Dudley, along with his coaches and teammates, boarded an airplane and flew hundreds of miles to find an opponent — an enemy, if you will — who tried to prevent them from taking the ball across that white chalk goal line.

"The tougher the enemy, the more intense the battle, the greater the thrill of victory," he said.

He and his teammates were never pleased if the opponent was weak, had no effective game plan and was unable to perform with skill. The real thrill of victory came when they had beaten the most formidable foe, knowing they had prepared well and executed the game plan — giving their best and coming home with the victory.

So it is in spiritual warfare. We have the most formidable

foe imaginable in Satan and his legions of demons. And there is no question we have the right coaches and equipment: God the Father, God the Son and God the Holy Spirit, along with all the spiritual armor and the direction of the Word through the revelation and inspiration of the Holy Spirit.

As I come to the close of this book, *Winning the Real War*, once again I would like to use the recent war in the Persian Gulf to illustrate spiritual truth.

As believers we are engaged this moment in mortal, spiritual combat. Satan not only wars against our souls, but he is actually opposing God Himself. The real war is between God and Satan, who has said, "I will ascend to heaven; I will raise my throne above the stars of God,...I will make myself like the Most High" (Is. 14:13-14).

Satan is fighting the eternal purposes and will of God. He is recruiting His own troops and seeking to destroy God's family. In order to defeat the church, the enemy forces must deceive, distract, divide and conquer. Thus far he has succeeded, but his days of success are coming to an end. God is raising up an army to stand united in spirit, sanctified in truth, unshakable, without fear, fighting the good fight of faith and storming the very gates of hell to set captives free all over the world.

Jesus came to seek and save the lost, to set free those in bondage and demonstrate the power of the gospel.[1] It is this purpose Satan fiercely opposes.

World evangelism is God's eternal purpose, and the powers of darkness are totally committed to halting this outreach. But God has chosen to announce "through the church to the rulers and the authorities in the heavenly places...the eternal purpose which He carried out in Christ

Jesus our Lord" (Eph. 3:10-11).

God is commanding every true believer to "awaken from sleep," "not participate in the unfruitful deeds of darkness," "stand firm," "make the most of your time," proclaim the gospel not in word only "but in demonstration of the Spirit and of power," be witnesses in all the earth and announce the victory as overcomers in this life.[2]

As surely as Saddam Hussein was defeated and Kuwait liberated by the united allied forces, so will Satan be defeated and those in captivity be set free for all eternity.

The Lord Jesus will come to claim a victorious bride, moving in harmony with His will, blameless and adorned in His abiding glory. You as a believer are a part of the body of Christ and must now become a vital part in fulfilling the Great Commission before He returns. It is for this purpose and this Person that we now live. Christ will come suddenly, but we have fixed our eyes on Him and are looking for His glorious appearing. As a prepared people we are fighting "the good fight of faith," that all the world may know the Lord Jesus in all of His fullness.[3]

Through us God will in the last days pour out His spirit on all flesh.[4] World evangelism will become a present reality.

Let us now go forth "more than conquerors"[5] to win the victory in this lifetime so we may bring glory and honor to the Lord Jesus Christ, our King of kings.

Scripture Abbreviations

Book	Abbreviation
Genesis	Gen.
Exodus	Ex.
Leviticus	Lev.
Numbers	Num.
Deuteronomy	Deut.
Joshua	Josh.
Judges	Judg.
Ruth	Ruth
First Samuel	1 Sam.
Second Samuel	2 Sam.
First Kings	1 Kin.
Second Kings	2 Kin.
First Chronicles	1 Chr.
Second Chronicles	2 Chr.
Ezra	Ezra
Nehemiah	Neh.
Esther	Esth.
Job	Job
Psalms	Ps.
Proverbs	Prov.
Ecclesiastes	Eccl.
Song of Solomon	Song
Isaiah	Is.
Jeremiah	Jer.
Lamentations	Lam.
Ezekiel	Ezek.
Daniel	Dan.
Hosea	Hos.
Joel	Joel
Amos	Amos

Obadiah ....Obad.
Jonah..Jon.
Micah..Mic.
Nahum...Nah.
Habakkuk ....Hab.
Zephaniah ....Zeph.
Haggai ....Hag.
Zechariah ....Zech.
Malachi..Mal.
Matthew ....Matt.
Mark..Mark
Luke ....Luke
John ....John
Acts ....Acts
Romans..Rom.
First Corinthians...1 Cor.
Second Corinthians...2 Cor.
Galatians ....Gal.
Ephesians ....Eph.
Philippians..Phil.
Colossians ....Col.
First Thessalonians...1 Thess.
Second Thessalonians...2 Thess.
First Timothy..1 Tim.
Second Timothy..2 Tim.
Titus..Titus
Philemon ....Philem.
Hebrews..Heb.
James ....James
First Peter..1 Pet.
Second Peter..2 Pet.
First John ....1 John
Second John ....2 John
Third John ....3 John
Jude ....Jude
Revelation...Rev.

NOTES

Introduction

1. See 2 Timothy 2:3; 1 Timothy 6:12; Romans 8:37.

Chapter 3

1. Quote by Francis Frangipane; used by permission.

Chapter 4

1. From tape transcript of television interview with Jerry Johnston, aired on "Restoration," July 24-25, 1989; James Robison Evangelistic Association; used by permission.
2. *Ibid.*
3. *Ibid.*
4. From tape transcript of television interview with Michael Haynes, Ph.D., aired on "Restoration," July 13 and 17, 1989; James Robison Evangelistic Association; used by permission.
5. *Ibid.*

Conclusion

1. See Luke 19:10; Luke 4:18; 1 Corinthians 2:4.
2. See Romans 13:11 (KJV); Ephesians 5:11; Ephisians 5:16; 1 Corinthians 2:4; Acts 1:7-8; 1 John 2:13-14.
3. See Hebrews 12:2 (KJV); Titus 2:13; 1 Timothy 6:12.

4. See Joel 2:28.
5. See Romans 8:37.